Children's Book Corner

Children's Book Corner

A READ-ALOUD Resource

with Tips, Techniques, and Plans
for Teachers, Librarians, and Parents

Level Grades 1 and 2

Judy Bradbury

Photographs by Gene Bradbury

LIBRARIES
U N L I M I T E D
A Member of the Greenwood Publishing Group

Westport, Connecticut • London

British Library Cataloguing in Publication Data is available.

Copyright © 2004 by Judy Bradbury

All rights reserved. No portion of this book may be reproduced, by any process or technique, without the express written consent of the publisher.

ISBN: 1-59158-047-1

First published in 2004

Libraries Unlimited, 88 Post Road West, Westport, CT 06881
A Member of the Greenwood Publishing Group, Inc.
www.lu.com

Printed in the United States of America

The paper used in this book complies with the Permanent Paper Standard issued by the National Information Standards Organization (Z39.48–1984).

10 9 8 7 6 5 4 3 2 1

Dedication

For Viola Grandinetti, "Aunt Lola," first of the DiRuscio girls, family historian, bang cutter, and role model to all her nieces: Thank you for showing us all what we are capable of and insisting we step up to the plate;

and

For Gene, my heartthrob and my anchor, and the father of the best kid I know: Thank you for always being there and for your steadfast commitment to what matters most. Have I told you lately . . . ?

Contents

Acknowledgments

This second book in the Children's Book Corner series was in some ways much more gratifying to pull together than the first, and in some ways much more daunting. The tough part came in making sure I didn't trip over any of the piles and piles of books that teetered on tables, in corners, in hallways, and in closets as I read, made lists, read, ordered more titles, read, and selected books to feature in the Read-aloud Plans and to reference in the Book Notes. The satisfying part came in knowing that teachers, librarians, and parents who were familiar with the first book in the series were enthusiastic and supportive. Their eagerness to offer title suggestions and resources helped make the writing and reading days all the more worthwhile. Their zeal bolstered my spirit.

A special nod of thanks go to Sharon Scott, Diana Smith, and Wendy Boyle of Trinikids Preschool, East Amherst, New York, my charter cheerleaders; Ann Mangan, teacher, parent, and friend whose shelves of children's books rival mine; Christine Bradford, parent, teacher, and director of the Empire Home School Group, and a woman whose energy, insight, dedication, and spirit are an inspiration; Wendy Pressman, teacher and parent, who willingly loaned me her impressive personal library of books about Hanukkah on the day before the holiday began (I returned them the next day, much to her children's relief.); Peg Papia, first-grade teacher at Saint Gregory the Great School, Williamsville, New York, whose reputation as a kind and involved teacher was not the least bit exaggerated; and Kay Kempner, first-grade teacher at Maple East Elementary School, Williamsville, New York, whose phone messages were so upbeat I'd leave them on the machine and replay them for days when I needed a boost.

On the other end of the project are the good people at Libraries Unlimited and Greenwood Publishing, whose enthusiasm for and support of this project are reflected in their professionalism and dedication to putting forward a top-notch package. Their efforts are deeply appreciated, and I look forward to new adventures as we work to figure out how to access a live person at online bookstores, and which latest and greatest camera is the best one for the project's photo shoots. Special thanks to graphic designer Mike Florman, marketing maven Erin Durkin, and my clear-thinking and most efficient editor, Sharon Coatney. Thank you all for making this project what it is by your various gifts of goodwill and dedication to your life work.

While it is not their life work, this project takes over the lives of those closest to me as it threatens to put home-cooked meals, clean socks and undies, and milk in the fridge on the endangered list. Thank you, Kelsey and Gene, for always managing to find a way to smile as you said, "No problem. Water is good. Barefoot works." I'm back.

Introduction

This resource book contains over fifty read-aloud plans for outstanding books to read with children in first and second grades. Hundreds of related titles are highlighted following the read-aloud plans and in the Book Notes section of this resource. There are fiction as well as nonfiction titles. Look for holiday selections, books on popular themes and content area subjects, biographies, poetry anthologies, and books about friends, pets, and family. Issues such as death, divorce, and facing bullies are addressed with the best there is to offer in bibliotherapy.

But most of all, these books can be classified as those that celebrate reading by the very excellence they bring to the picture book and early chapter book form. They are meant to nourish the spirit and encourage the beginning and newly independent reader to embrace the wonderful world of reading.

In addition to Read-Aloud Plans, you will find Tips and Techniques for Teachers and Librarians, Parent Pull-out Pages intended to be sent home every few weeks throughout the school year, and an extensive Book Notes section that lists hundreds of titles by subject with a brief summary of each. Finally, look for subject, title, author, and illustrator indexes to help you find just the right book for a special group or particular child.

How Were the Choices Made About Which Books to Include?

In deciding which children's books to include in this resource, several criteria were used to determine whether the book would be highlighted with a read-aloud plan, listed in the Book Notes, mentioned on a Parent Pull-Out Page, or not included in the resource at all. The determination was based on several factors, the most important of which was whether the book told an original story in an appealing way with art that successfully merged with the text to create a memorable package for the first- and second-grade child. I strove to introduce worthy titles, both new and older, that teachers, librarians, and parents might not be familiar with, rather than well-known classics or popular children's titles. However, a list of titles children of this age should not miss is included in the Parent Pull-Out Pages. These books ought to be the foundation of your read-aloud program and the cornerstone of every classroom and school library. Similarly, there is an extensive list of beginning reader books that will encourage and stimulate young readers, as well as a listing of chapter books that are ideal for reading aloud.

What Do I Need to Know to Find the Book?

Publication information is provided for each book for which there is a read-aloud plan. This reflects the most up-to-date information available at the time of the printing of *Children's Book Corner*. As there are a number of editions available for most titles, from hardcover to softcover to library binding, I have listed the hardcover edition publication information unless the book is not available in hardcover. By referring to the title information and looking up its listing in library catalogs, online bookstores, or publisher catalogs or Web sites, you can access information on the edition that best suits your needs.

Which Edition Should I Get?

There are typically several editions available for each of the titles presented here. The edition you choose will be based on your needs, budget, and purposes. If you are trying out a book, plan to use it just once, or have a limited budget, consider borrowing the title from the public library. If the school library owns it, you're in luck! Should you decide to purchase books, consider which edition will work best for you.

Hardcover editions are the most common and most durable for use in the classroom library. Although they cost more initially than softcover copies, they will last longer and will not need to be replaced as often.

Library binding editions are especially designed for longer shelf life as in library settings, but these sturdy editions can be perfect for the classroom library as well. As they tend to be a bit more expensive, you may want to choose this edition for those books in the classroom library that you think will see the most use over an extended length of time.

Softcover editions are ideal for schools with limited budgets and for multiple-copy purchases for classrooms that offer a library-lending program for students and their families. Special printings of books are arranged by school book clubs and appear in softcover (and sometimes specially priced hardbound) editions available for purchase at very reasonable prices only through that club and usually only for a limited time.

Each edition bears its own ISBN, so be sure to note the correct one when ordering books for purchase.

How Do I Know What the Book Is About?

In addition to publication information, you will find subject categories listed for each book. Use this handy reference when you are trying to find just the right title to augment a unit of study, a particular season, or an issue you want to explore with your children. The subject index provided at the back of the book will help with this search as well.

How Does the Read-Aloud Plan Work?

Each plan follows the same format. At the top is the publication information and an estimate of the actual time it ought to take to read the book aloud (NOT including questions and follow-up activities, as these are used at the reader's discretion and the time spent on them will vary). Next you will find a brief summary of the book. The teaching plan itself consists of three parts.

The read-aloud session begins with a *Prereading Focus.* The plan suggests ways to introduce the book. This is an important step in the read-aloud plan because it focuses the child on the book, its format, and its subject. Discussion before reading aids in building prediction skills and nurtures experiential background by enabling children to draw on their personal experiences to bring meaning to the story. As children discuss and answer questions, they verbalize thoughts and feelings and relate their experiences. Each read-aloud plan launches the reading of the book with a "let's read to find out" focus for listening to the story.

In the *While Reading* portion of the read-aloud plan, you will find questions to pose as you read the book aloud. Answers are given in parentheses to even the simplest and most obvious questions for ease in following the plan while preparing in advance for the read-aloud session. Suggestions for reading the book aloud specific to that title also will be found in this section.

The *Follow-Up Discussion* offers ideas for bringing the read-aloud session to a meaningful close. Questions that relate to the outcome of the story are posed. Discussion is encouraged. On some of the plans you will find additional information about related titles, the author, the illustrator, or both, that you may want to share with children, and suggested follow-up activities that extend beyond a simple follow-up. Related books are briefly described. Occasionally "book words," such as "illustrator," or terms important to the story are presented. Introduce these words in context rather than as isolated "vocabulary."

It is advisable to become familiar with the read-aloud plan as well as the book prior to presenting it to children. While you may want to have the plan handy and may wish to highlight particular questions on the plan that you want to be sure to ask, it is not advisable to follow the plan line by line as the book is being read aloud. This will affect your presentation, which ought to be smooth, uninterrupted, and delivered in a confident and prepared manner.

Note: Have an easel with chart paper or a board available in the read-aloud area. Many of the plans suggest follow-up activities that make use of these. A mini-glossary of book terms used in the plans can be found at the back of the book for your reference.

How Do You Recommend I Use the Questions Provided in the Plans?

When asking the suggested questions, rephrase children's answers into complete sentences. Reinforce responses by beginning with an affirmative. For example, if the question is, "What is the duck wearing?" and the response you get is, "an orange hat!" respond with: "Yes, Erin, the duck has an orange hat on his head." If the answer you get is, "feathers," you might respond with, "Yes, Erin, the duck has lots of feathers, doesn't she? What is she wearing?" If a response is incorrect or not what you are after, accept the answer and rephrase the question. Avoid negative responses ("No, that's not right.") .

When asking children to relate personal experiences, be flexible within reason and allow for variance. If the discussion gets off track, try this: "That's interesting, Jake. Now can you tell me what tricks your dog can do?" or "I see, your dog is brown and has long fur. Does he know any tricks?" When you are seeking a specific response, allow children to throw out answers and prompt with, "Yes, anything else?" or "I hadn't thought about that! Any other ideas?" To bring kids back to the topic at hand, say, "I'll take one more answer and then we will go on."

Several questions are suggested in each part of the read-aloud plan. You are encouraged to use some or all according to your schedule, the attention span of your children, and their needs as you perceive them. You may want to use some questions on the initial reading and leave others for repeated readings. Reading a book more than once is strongly encouraged. Repeated readings do not require prereading or while reading development, as children are already familiar with the story. Repeated readings develop a deeper awareness and sense of the meaning of the story, make books feel comfortable and familiar, encourage modeling behavior, and foster emergent reading skills.

What Is the Purpose of the Parent Pull-Out Pages?

In this section of the book you will find material developed especially for parents or caregivers responsible for the children with whom you work. Permission is granted to reproduce the Parent Pull-Out Pages for distribution. It is recommended that these pages be sent home every few weeks throughout the school year. Their purpose is to reinforce the importance of reading aloud to children, to provide useful information to parents and caregivers in an effort to turn belief into practice, and to demystify the principles of beginning reading instruction. It is essential to drive home the key role parents play in early reading instruction.

How Should I Use the Tips and Techniques for Teachers and Librarians Section of the Book?

This portion of the book is designed to provide practical suggestions for professionals who work with beginning readers and newly independent readers. Resources, tips, and techniques are presented in the hope that teachers and librarians will utilize this section of the book as needed and find it to be a handy reference tool.

What Will I Find in the Book Notes?

This section of the book offers hundreds of additional titles according to subject, with a brief summary of each. Bibliographic information is also included.

Why So Many Indexes?

Subject, title, author, and illustrator indexes are provided at the back of the book for your convenience in locating the information you need on just the right book quickly and with ease. Use these indexes when you need to locate information on every book included in this resource.

What If I Have Questions, Comments, or Feedback?

I'd love to hear from you! If you have information you'd like to share with me or would like to arrange a school visit, parent program, or teacher in-service training, send an e-mail to my attention at judyreads@bluefrog.com. Place "Children's Book Corner" in the subject line, please, so you'll be sure it reaches me. For information on other books in the Children's Book Corner series, visit www.lu.com.

Read-Aloud Plans

Title . . . . IRA SLEEPS OVER
Author/Illustrator . . . . Bernard Waber
Publisher . . . . Houghton Mifflin
Copyright Date 1972
Ages 5–7
Read-Aloud Time . . . . 6–8 minutes
Subject . . . Sleepovers, self-esteem, self-confidence, friends

Oh boy, is Ira excited! Tonight will be his first-ever sleepover. But wait . . . will Reggie laugh at him if he brings along his bedtime buddy?

So begins IRA SLEEPS OVER, written and illustrated by Bernard Waber. Known for his portrayal of sensitive characters meeting ordinary, everyday problems, Waber has written dozens of picture books for children, many of them about Lyle the Crocodile. What makes this book worth noting is its subtle examination of peer pressure.

Throughout this tale we tag along with Ira as he wanders through the neighborhood pondering whether to take Tah Tah, his teddy bear, along on his sleepover. His mother and father feel certain Reggie will not laugh at him. His sister, however, is only too happy to discourage her younger brother. From her perch atop the piano bench, she predicts that Reggie most certainly will laugh at him. And so, Tah Tah stays at home. How Ira ends up sleeping peacefully in Reggie's room with Tah Tah in his arms and his problem solved is the essence of this simply written and delightfully illustrated story.

IRA SLEEPS OVER provides a humorous, nonthreatening introduction to the issue of peer pressure and being true to oneself. It helps the listener realize that each of us is not all that different from our friends or classmates. Through an amusing story, Waber provides insight into a problem that has touched us all at one time or another. This is the book to reach for when a child is hesitant to be himself. This is the book to read again when his self-confidence needs bolstering. I know. I've read it to my teddy bear countless times.

> **PREREADING FOCUS:** Ask: What is a sleepover? Why is a sleepover fun? Would you like to go on a sleepover? To whose house? What would you bring with you? Do you have a favorite stuffed animal you like to sleep with? Would you bring it on a sleepover? Why/why not? **Let's read to find out** what Ira does when he is invited for a sleepover.

> **WHILE READING:** Draw attention to the subtle details of the artwork that help us to know what the main character and supporting cast are thinking and feeling. Draw conclusions.

> **FOLLOW-UP DISCUSSION:** Ask: Did you like the ending? Why? How do you know Ira felt better with Tah Tah than without him? If you were Ira, would you have taken Tah Tah to Reggie's for the sleepover in the first place? Why do you think

Ira took his sister's advice instead of his mom and dad's? Would you have laughed at Ira if he brought Tah Tah to your house for a sleepover? Do you think Reggie will bring Foo Foo to Ira's house for a sleepover? What do you think Ira will do the next time he goes on a sleepover?

IRA SLEEPS OVER. Reprinted by permission of Houghton Mifflin.

Notes:

Title . . . . DABBLE DUCK
Author . . . . Anne Leo Ellis
Illustrator . . . . Sue Truesdell
Publisher . . . . HarperCollins
Copyright Date 1984
Ages . . . . 5–8 years
Read-Aloud Time . . . . 7–8 minutes
Subject . . . . Pets, city life

DABBLE DUCK is delightful. It is the story of an apartment duck and his best friend, Jason. The playful illustrations by Sue Truesdell complement the story line and are a pleasure in and of themselves. With splashes of bright color, they characterize Jason as a likable kid and Dabble as a duck we'd all love to have as a pet in our city apartment. (Did I really say that?!) There is an appealing attention to detail in the illustrations, from the sidewalk grocer who feeds Dabble a chunk of bread while holding back a hissing cat, to the final scene in which the characters are asleep in a bedroom strewn with toys, clothes, and a pair of rabbit slippers.

Jason's parents are refreshing characters, well-drawn by author Anne Leo Ellis. They are loving, supportive, and honest. An overall sense of warmth and goodness is reflected on the pages of this story about how Jason and Dabble solve the problem of Dabble's loneliness while Jason is away at school all day.

Chosen as a Reading Rainbow Book, DABBLE DUCK not only explores the values of a pet but also gives the reader a glimpse of big-city life. Here we see apartment living in a high-rise with crowded elevators, and a city park where nannies meet, pigeons convene, and sidewalk merchants sell hot dogs and popcorn. The reader encounters a thoroughly modern family, one that is successful in its attempt to be a unit that values its individual members' uniqueness. Hooray for that! Hooray for DABBLE DUCK, an enjoyable read-aloud for children ages five and up.

> **PREREADING FOCUS**: Ask: When you think of a pet, what do you think of? Who has an unusual house pet? Would a duck make a good house pet? Why/why not? Discuss. **Let's read to find out** about Dabble Duck, an apartment pet.

> **WHILE READING**: Enjoy the illustrations. Give attention to the myriad details that extend the story. Note elements and characteristics of city life.

> **FOLLOW-UP DISCUSSION**: Ask: Do you think Quack is a good name for the dog? Why? Do you think Dabble will be happy now? How is Jason's home, street, neighborhood, different from yours? How is it the same? What are some other unlikely household pets?

For another warm and fuzzy choosing-a-pet story, consider "LET'S GET A PUP!" SAID KATE, by Bob Graham (Candlewick). For a gentle story based on true events about a stray cat, see GO HOME! THE TRUE STORY OF JAMES THE CAT, by Libby Phillips Meggs (Whitman).

For additional books about pets, refer to Book Notes.

Notes:

Title	THE POLAR EXPRESS
Author/Illustrator	Chris Van Allsburg
Publisher	Houghton Mifflin
Ages	6 and up
Copyright Date	1985
Read-Aloud Time	8–10 minutes
Subject	Christmas

Note: Have a shiny, tinkly bell on hand when reading this book aloud. (See notes below.) Consider encouraging children to wear pajamas on the day a read-aloud of this book is planned and offering nougat candies or hot chocolate at the appropriate time in the story.

Christmastime. This season more than any other sparks nostalgia, stirs familial yearnings, creates magic, and bids a festive spirit. It is at once gentle, joyful, and hopeful. It is the season for believing.

True to the spirit of the season is the classic picture book, THE POLAR EXPRESS, which is itself magical, gentle, and hopeful. Widely acclaimed, it was the recipient in 1986 of the prestigious Caldecott Award, which honors the most distinguished American picture book published each year. This book is as much for adults (or maybe more so than) as it is for children. But make no mistake; children love it, too. They just may interpret it differently.

Created by author-illustrator Chris Van Allsburg, THE POLAR EXPRESS tells of a boy's Christmas Eve adventure. The superb full-color illustrations are ethereal and dreamlike. They beckon us to follow the child as he climbs aboard a magical train bound for the North Pole. Over mountains and through frozen wilderness we go, willingly, longingly, expectantly, and we are not disappointed. We are there amid countless elves when the boy is chosen to receive the first gift of Christmas. We are there when the treasure is lost, and when it is found again on Christmas morning. And in the end we learn the secret of keeping the magic alive in this, the season for believing.

PREREADING FOCUS: Enjoy the book's cover. Ask: What does the word *polar* make you think of? What about the word *express*? What do you think this book is about? What season of the year is it? What holidays are celebrated in the winter? Where do you think the train might be going? Have you ever heard the sound a small silver bell makes? Can you describe it? (Ring your bell!) **Let's read to find out** what a bell has to do with this story.

WHILE READING: Ask: How do you think the boy feels as he climbs aboard the Polar Express? Have nougat candies or hot chocolate? Distribute after reading the page on which these are mentioned. Ask: Would you like to ride on the Polar Express? Who do you think will receive the first gift of Christmas? On the page where all the elves gathered, ask for estimates of how many elves there are. After reading what the boy asks for, ask: What would you ask for if you were the boy?

FOLLOW-UP DISCUSSION: Ask: How does this story make you feel? Explain. What does the boy long to hear in the beginning of the story? Do you think you'd like to ride on the Polar Express? How do you think the boy felt when Santa Claus chose him to receive the first gift of Christmas? The boy chooses a silver bell from Santa's sleigh. Why? What would you have chosen? The silver bell is lost. Where does the boy find it? How do you think it got there? Who is "Mr. C."? Why couldn't the boy's parents hear the silver bell? In the end, why can the boy still hear the bell even though he has grown older?

Available in hardcover, paperback, and gift sets that include a bell, a train car, a tape, a CD, or a combination of these!

For two other Christmas classics, don't miss THE CHRISTMAS MIRACLE OF JONATHAN TOOMEY, written by Susan Wojciechowski and illustrated by P. J. Lynch (Candlewick), in which a widow, her son, and a sad woodcarver make for joy and a miracle, and SANTA CALLS, by William Joyce (HarperCollins), a Christmas fantasy like no other.

For additional holiday titles, see Book Notes.

THE POLAR EXPRESS. Reprinted by permission of Houghton Mifflin.

Notes:

Title	RUBY THE COPYCAT
Author/Illustrator	Peggy Rathmann
Publisher	Scholastic
Copyright Date	1991
Ages	5–8
Read-Aloud Time	6–8 minutes
Subject	Copycats, being yourself

Ruby is new to the class. But things are okay. Miss Hart seems nice, and she seats Ruby behind Angela and her red bow. Angela seems nice, too. She is friendly toward Ruby—for a while, that is—until she gets exasperated with Ruby for copying her all the time in every way. With bright, cheerful illustrations that enhance and extend the dry humor of the text, this story gently questions the wisdom of imitation as the best form of flattery. "You can be anything you want to be," says Miss Hart. "But be Ruby first. I like Ruby." And eventually Ruby hops to it.

This first picture book by the funny, warm, and fuzzy author/illustrator who went on to win a Caldecott Medal for OFFICER BUCKLE AND GLORIA (see read-aloud plan elsewhere in this book) demonstrates the dimension of interplay between text and illustration in a model picture book. From Ruby's expressive eyes to Angela's voluminous hair, to the perspective we have on Ruby as she heads home for lunch at noon each day, the story is rounded out and developed by the zesty illustrations. Not that the text is slight. "Wet paint," is all we need in one scene, while in another, Ruby "buried her chin in the collar of her blouse" and "Miss Hart folded her hands and looked very serious." Finely crafted from beginning to end, this book will tickle while it teaches, and what could be better than that?

> **PREREADING FOCUS:** Ask: What is a copycat? Do you like to be copied? Why? Why would someone want to copy someone else? Discuss. Today we are going to read the story of Ruby, who as you can see from the title, is a copycat. **Let's read to find out** who and what Ruby copies and what happens when she doesn't.

> **WHILE READING**: Pay particular attention to *how* Ruby copies, the subject of much of the humor in the illustrations. Draw attention to how Angela goes from friendly to exasperated and grouchy, her choice in outfits to match her mood (black), and the importance lunch recess has throughout the story.

> **FOLLOW-UP DISCUSSION:** Ask: Why does Ruby copy Angela and Miss Hart? Why do you think Angela gets sore at Ruby? How would you feel if someone copied you all the time? What is a *coincidence*? (Refer back to text.) What advice does Miss Hart give Ruby? What do you think she means by this? How does Ruby copy Miss Hart? What does Ruby decide? (To stop copying others.)

How can you tell? (She removes the fingernails.) In the end, Ruby doesn't copy anyone. What does she do? (Hops.) What happens? (Everyone copies her!) Do you think Angela is mad at Ruby anymore? (No.) How do you know? (They hop off together.) What is the funniest thing Ruby does when she is copying Angela? If you decided to copy one thing someone else does, what would it be? What might others copy that you do?

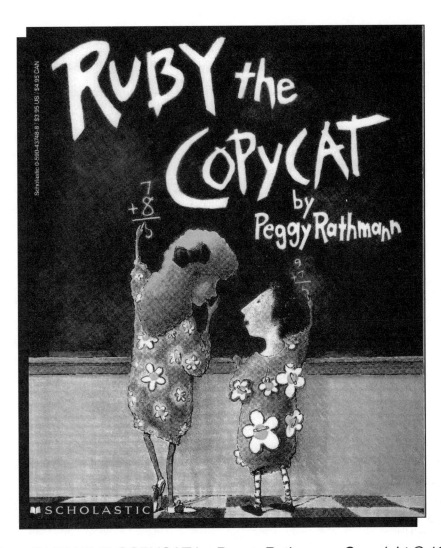

*From RUBY THE COPYCAT by Peggy Rathmann. Copyright © 1991
by Margaret Rathman. Used by permission of Scholastic Inc.*

Notes:

Title	THE BEAR'S BICYCLE
Author	Emilie Warren McLeod
Illustrator	David McPhail
Publisher	Little, Brown
Copyright Date	1986
Ages	5–7
Read-Aloud Time	6–8 minutes
Subject	Bicycle safety, imaginary friends

It's delightful how skilled illustrator David McPhail was able to take this straightforward bike safety "slice of life" story and turn it into a keeper. Read the words alone, and it's a day in the life of a boy who loves to ride his bike and knows how to be responsible on wheels. He's careful and conscientious, explaining the rules of safety, checking the tires and brakes before setting out, and pulling his bike into the garage before it gets dark.

But the bear, on the other hand, is classic alter ego. While the little guy is steering around cans and broken glass, the roly-poly rapscallion is kicking the can, and while the cautious kid stays to the right when he meets another bike, the barreling bundle of bravado is wreaking havoc on the path to destruction.

It's the last few spreads, though, that I like best. The milk and crackers, the paw prints on the kitchen floor, the bandage strategically placed. And the last page . . . well, it just doesn't get any better than that. Don't miss this one.

> **PREREADING FOCUS:** Let's talk about bicycles. Ask: What should we remember as we go out riding? On chart paper or the chalkboard, list safety rules children suggest. Show the cover of the book. Read the title. **Let's read to find out** about this bear's bike ride. Show the title page. Discuss the details found in the illustration.

> **WHILE READING:** Revel in the illustrations that tell a parallel story to the text. Note hand signals. Discuss why it's a good idea to get off your bike when crossing a street. Ask: Why do we stay to the right when we meet other bikes? Briefly discuss the rules presented on each page and note the infractions of the wild and woolly title character. Point out the details on the final pages (footprints, stuffed animal, bandage).

> **FOLLOW-UP DISCUSSION:** Return to the title page and note details of the two bikes in the garage and the boy and stuffed bear in the window. Check out the back cover, too. Review the list of bicycle safety rules generated by the group. Add rules learned as a result of reading the book.

Note: This character does not wear a bike helmet. Stress the importance of always wearing a helmet when riding a bike.

For another comical look at safety rules, see the read-aloud plan for OFFICER BUCKLE AND GLORIA, by Peggy Rathmann (Putnam) found elsewhere in this part of this book.

Notes:

Title	Q IS FOR DUCK
Author	Mary Elting and Michael Folsom
Illustrator	Jack Kent
Publisher	Clarion
Copyright Date	1980
Ages	5–7
Read-Aloud Time	8–10 minutes
Subject	Beginning letter sounds, guessing game, prediction

Note: Some preparation is required for the Follow-Up activity. See notes below.

You can tell from the title of this book what slant the authors have taken on the approach to letters and the sounds they make. **Q** is for duck because . . . "a duck **q**uacks." Likewise, "**F** is for bird . . . because a bird **f**lies." The lighthearted approach to teaching letter sounds is reflected not only in the format but also in the comical line drawings. Readers must turn the page to find out whether their prediction is correct. And most of the time it will be, as the game is geared for positive reinforcement peppered with laughs from A to Z. My favorite is "**S** is for camel . . . ." Go see!

PREREADING FOCUS: Introduce this book by telling the children that today we are going to read an alphabet book that's different from most other alphabet books. Show the cover. Ask: What letter is this? Read the title. Ask: Why do you think **Q** is for duck? **Let's read to find out** what the other letters of the alphabet stand for.

WHILE READING: This book is perfect for making predictions. Utilize the format to get the most from the material. Encourage children to predict what the next page will show. Make full use of the picture clues. Enunciate the sound of the letter that will be reinforced by the illustration on the following page.

FOLLOW-UP DISCUSSION: Ask children which page is their favorite and why. Assign a letter to each child. (You may want to prepare beforehand a set of index cards or tagboard with an upper- and lowercase letter of the alphabet printed on them.) Ideally, you will cover every letter of the alphabet. Have children fold a piece of drawing paper in half. On the front flap, each child will write: [letter] *is for* . . . . Ask children to draw a picture on the inside spread and label it in the style of the book. Attach index cards. When they have finished, ask children to help you put the pages in order. Construct a classroom book from the pages the children have created or display the artwork clockwise around the room from A to Z!

For another book with an unusual approach to the alphabet, letter sounds, and rhyme, look for NONSENSE! HE YELLED, written by Roger Eschbacher and illustrated by Adrian Johnson (Dial).

Q IS FOR DUCK. Reprinted by permission of Houghton Mifflin.

Notes:

Title . . . . CLICK, CLACK, MOO: COWS THAT TYPE	
Author . . . . Doreen Cronin	
Illustrator . . . . Betsy Lewin	
Publisher . . . . Simon & Schuster	
Copyright Date 2000	
Ages 5–7	
Read-Aloud Time . . . . 6–8 minutes	
Subject . . . . Writing as communication, farm animals	

Note: If you have access to a manual typewriter, make arrangements to have it on hand when you present this book!

Farmer Brown is grouchy. His darn cows are punctuating their moos with "click, clack, click, clack, clickity clack." And as if all the racket's not enough, they're posting notes on the barnyard door demanding . . . electric blankets! When Farmer Brown says no, they say no milk. When the chickens join in, then there's no milk and no eggs, despite Farmer Brown's written demands. When they finally make a deal, things are just ducky.

PREREADING FOCUS: Ask: Have you ever written a note or a letter? Discuss. Have you ever typed a note or letter or written an e-mail on the computer? Does anyone know what a "typewriter" is? Let's break the word apart. What does a "writer" do? What does it mean to "type"? Now what do you think the word "typewriter" means? (Explain that a typewriter was used before computers and keyboards.) A typewriter is pictured on the cover and back flap. Ask: What does it sound like when you type on a computer keyboard? Explain that a typewriter sounds like a keyboard, only louder and sharper because you have to hit the keys hard to make an impression on a piece of paper rolled onto a cartridge above the keys. (Demonstrate if you have a typewriter!) Show the cover of the book. These cows are using a typewriter. Ask: What do you think they are doing? (Writing a letter.) Whom might they be writing to? What might the letter be about? What else do you see on the cover? (Rooster, duck.) Where do you think this story takes place? (On a farm.) **Let's read to find out** what and why the cows are typing.

WHILE READING: After the first few pages, ask: Why do you think Farmer Brown is unhappy with the cows? What does "go on strike" mean? Draw attention to and discuss the illustration with the farmer's shadow in the background. Farmer Brown is furious when the hens go on strike. Ask the children what they think Farmer Brown ought to do. Elicit predictions of what will happen next. Read through Duck's entrance in the story. Ask what "a neutral party" might be. (One who doesn't take sides.) What do you think an "ultimatum" is? (A demand.) Read on. When Farmer Brown gets the animals' counteroffer, ask what they think he will do. Read the next spread. Ask: Why do you think Farmer Brown decided this was a good deal? What do you think will happen now? Read to the end.

FOLLOW-UP DISCUSSION: Ask: Is Duck successful? (Yes.) What do you think will happen next on Farmer Brown's farm? Read the sequel to this Caldecott Honor Book, GIGGLE, GIGGLE, QUACK! (Simon & Schuster) to find out. That one's just ducky, too.

For another book on the power of correspondence, see the read-aloud plan for DEAR MRS. LARUE LETTERS FROM OBEDIENCE SCHOOL, by Mark Teague (Scholastic). For an enjoyable introduction to punctuation, reach for PUNCTUATION TAKES A VACATION, written by Robin Pulver and illustrated by Lynn Rowe Reed (Holiday House). See the read-aloud plan. Refer to Tips and Techniques for Teachers and Librarians and Book Notes for more writing-related read-aloud suggestions.

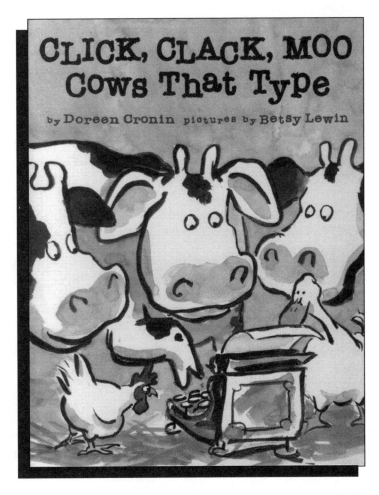

Text and illustrations copyright © 2000 CLICK CLACK MOO: COWS THAT TYPE written by Doreen Cronin and illustrated by Betsy Lewin.
Used with permission of Simon & Schuster Books for Young Readers, a division of Simon & Schuster Children's Publishing.

Notes:

Title	THE COFFEE CAN KID
Author	Jan M. Czech
Illustrator	Maurie J. Manning
Publisher	Child & Family Press
Copyright Date	2002
Ages	5–8
Read-Aloud Time	6–8 minutes
Subject	Foreign adoption, family

Note: To prepare for the reading of this story, place a baby photo and a "letter" in a coffee can. Have the coffee can on hand as you begin the story.

Based on the experience of adopting her own Korean-born daughter, Czech brings warmth and affirmation to this story of love at first sight between parent and child. The illustrations complement the text and heighten the feeling of rightness and unconditional love. Woven through the story are facts found not only in a coffee can preserving a letter and a birth photo but also in the heart of a parent—regardless of culture or circumstance. "The coffee can kid was the most beautiful baby in the world," says the father. "There was a problem, though." So begins the story.

PREREADING FOCUS: Hold up a coffee can. Ask: What could you keep in a coffee can? The title of this book is COFFEE CAN KID. Show cover. Ask: What do you think the title means? **Let's read to find out** who the coffee can kid is and why she is called that.

WHILE READING: On page 1, ask: What is Annie trying to reach? (Coffee can.) What do you think might be in the can? Listen as I read to find out more about Annie. Note the environment, the cultural clues, and the birth mom's emotions as you read through the story.

FOLLOW-UP DISCUSSION: Ask: How old is Annie? (Six.) Where was she born? (In a hut in the country in an unspecified Asian country.) What is a "hut"? (Small, simple shelter; shack.) Where does she live now? (America.) What does Dong Hee mean? (Shining Hope.) Which name would you rather have—Shining Hope or Annie? Why? Who is the coffee can kid? (Annie.) Why is she the coffee can kid? (Her birth photo and a letter from her birth mother are kept in a coffee can.) Why can't Annie's father read the letter to her? (It's written in another language.) Why is it kept in a can? (It's the best way to keep the photo from fading.) Why do you think that Annie wants the coffee can to sit on a lower shelf? (So she can reach it more easily.) How does Annie feel at the end of the story? What are two things that the contents of the coffee can sound like to Annie? (Fall leaves and butterfly wings.) Do you think it sounds like that? Demonstrate! What else do a photo and a letter in a coffee can sound like?

Related titles: THE WHITE SWAN EXPRESS: A STORY ABOUT ADOPTION, written by Jean Davies Okimoto and Elaine M. Aoki, illustrated by Meilo So (Clarion); HAPPY ADOPTION DAY!, lyrics by John McCutcheon, illustrated by Julie Paschkis (Little, Brown); TELL ME AGAIN ABOUT THE NIGHT I WAS BORN, written by Jamie Lee Curtis, illustrated by Laura Cornell (HarperCollins); OVER THE MOON: AN ADOPTION TALE, by Karen Katz (Holt).

Cover of THE COFFEE CAN KID, copyright 2002 by Maurie J. Manning, reprinted with permission.

Notes:

Title	TODAY WAS A TERRIBLE DAY
Author	Patricia Reilly Giff
Illustrator	Susanna Natti
Publisher	Viking
Copyright Date	1980
Ages	5–7
Read-Aloud Time	5–7 minutes
Subject	Having a bad day, learning to read

Everybody has a bad day now and then. But Ronald Morgan's bad day would make the record books. He drops his pencil, and it's downhill from there. Things go from bad to worse as he sneaks a sandwich from the wrong lunch bag, forges his mother's signature only to spell her name wrong, misses a fly ball at recess, can't do his workbook page, and knocks over Miss Tyler's BIG plant. It doesn't help, either, that he "can't read." But when Miss Tyler gives him a note to take home and he reads it *all by himself*, things start looking up. Lucky for Ronald, lucky for teachers who need to bolster the troops, and lucky for the troops treated to this story.

PREREADING FOCUS: Ask: Have you ever had a terrible day? What happened? Did the day eventually get better? How? What are some things you can do when you're having a bad day? Discuss. Look at the cover. What do you see here? Where do you think this story takes place? (In school.) This is Ronald. What kind of day do you think he's having? This is Miss Tyler, Ronald's teacher. What kind of a day do you think she's having? Read the title. Who do you think is telling this story? **Let's read to find out** why today was a terrible day.

WHILE READING: Read the first few spreads. Ask: Who is having a bad day? (Ronald.) Why is it a bad day? How do you think Ronald feels when all the kids laugh? How do you think Ronald feels when Jimmy cries? How do you think Jimmy feels? How do you think Miss Tyler feels? Read until Ronald is returned to his classroom after the water fountain mishap. Ask: What have we found out about Ronald so far? (He has trouble in school with reading, among other things!) What nickname has Ronald picked up? (Snakey.) Why? (When Ronald dropped his pencil, Miss Tyler asked why he was crawling on the floor like a snake.) Do you think Ronald likes his nickname? (No.) Why? Would you like that nickname? Why? After the reading group scene, write the two sentences, "Sally was a horse" and "Sally saw a house" on chart paper. Ask children what words Ronald read incorrectly. Discuss. Read on. Ask: How does Ronald feel when he knocks over the plant? How does Miss Tyler feel? *Before* you read the contents of the note, ask: How does Ronald feel about getting a note to take home? (Dismayed.) How do you know? (Look at that face!) What do you think the note says? Read to the end of the story.

FOLLOW-UP DISCUSSION: Ask: How does Ronald feel after he *reads* the note? (Overjoyed.) Why does Ronald decide to give Miss Tyler a plant for her birthday? (It will replace the one he knocked over.) Is Ronald still having a terrible day? (No.) When do you think it changed? (When he read the note.) Has Ronald changed his mind about his nickname? (Yes.) How do you know? (He calls himself Snakey when he phones Michael.) What kind of day do you think Ronald and Miss Tyler will have tomorrow? (A happy day!)

For another humorous dose of a fabulously wise teacher, this time seen through the eyes of the popular young diva, dancer, ambulance driver, Lilly, reach for LILLY'S PURPLE PLASTIC PURSE, by Kevin Henkes (Greenwillow).

For another title about a bad day of epic proportions, see read-aloud plan for ALEXANDER AND THE TERRIBLE, HORRIBLE, NO GOOD, VERY BAD DAY, written by Judith Viorst and illustrated by Ray Cruz (Atheneum) found elsewhere in this resource.

Notes:

Title	AXLE ANNIE
Author	Robin Pulver
Illustrator	Tedd Arnold
Publisher	Puffin
Copyright Date	1999
Ages	5–8
Read-Aloud Time	5–7 minutes
Subject	Snow days, school bus drivers, a positive attitude, good deeds

The luckiest kids in the town of Burskyville ride on Axle Annie's school bus. And whenever a snowstorm is brewing, the superintendent of schools calls her to ask if he should close the schools because Tiger Hill, the toughest hill in town, is on her route. Axle Annie's answer is always the same. "Mr. Solomon! Do snowplows plow? Do tow trucks tow? Are school buses yellow? Of course I can make it up Tiger Hill!" And she always does. Shifty Rhodes, the nastiest school bus driver in Burskyville, grumbles that they never have a snow day, so he devises a plan. With colored pencil and watercolor washes, illustrator Tedd Arnold adds his distinctive brand of comedy to the hilarious text, which results in a treasure of a book that will have listeners wanting to head for Axle Annie Slope again and again.

PREREADING FOCUS: Show the cover of the book and read the title. Ask children who they think Axle Annie is. (Bus driver.) What kind of person does she seem to be? Note seasonal details on the cover and ask children to predict what the story is about. **Let's read to find out** more about Axle Annie.

WHILE READING: Read through the first several spreads until you get to Shifty Rhodes. Ask: How do the children feel about Axle Annie? (They love her.) Why? (She tells jokes, sings silly songs, calls out cheerfully, roars up Tiger Hill.) How do the townspeople feel about Axle Annie? (They love her, too.) Why? (She helps drivers stranded on Tiger Hill.) Read through the hatching of Shifty and Hale's plan to foil Axle Annie to the spread showing Shifty making his way to the bus in the "wingdinger of a storm." Ask: Will Axle Annie make it? Read on to the end of the story.

FOLLOW-UP DISCUSSION: Ask: How did Axle Annie make it up the hill? (All the stranded drivers she had helped in the past helped her.) What did Axle Annie always say when Mr. Solomon, the superintendent of schools, called her to ask if he should close the schools? (See above.) What do the children say as they ski down Axle Annie Slope? ("Do snowplows plow? Do tow trucks tow? Are school buses yellow? Of course we can make it down Axle Annie Slope!") Could this become the classroom mantra when times are tough?

For additional snowy showstoppers, try THE WILD TOBOGGAN RIDE, written by Suzan Reid and illustrated by Eugenie Fernandes (Scholastic), about a day on the hills, and SNOW DAY!, written by Patricia Lakin and illustrated by Scott Nash (Dial), in which the principals head for the hills with their toboggans! For more winter books, see Book Notes.

Notes:

Title . . . . CLEVER BEATRICE
Author . . . . Margaret Willey
Illustrator . . . . Heather Solomon
Publisher . . . . Atheneum
Copyright Date 2001
Ages 5–7
Read-Aloud Time . . . . 5–7 minutes
Subject . . . . . . Tall tale, wily wit triumphs over brainless brawn

Note: The Follow-Up activity suggested for this book requires preplanning and is extensive.

"Sure, she was little, but Beatrice loved riddles and tricks and she could think fast on her feet." So begins this charming Canadian tall tale known as a *conte*. While reading, refer back to the colorful inside cover and trace Clever Beatrice's path to the bag full of gold coins she earns for her mother. And earn it she does, outwitting the fearsome rich giant who likes to gamble on his strength. Clever, that girl. "Sharp as a tack," says her mother. Get ready to cheer.

PREREADING FOCUS: Ask: What does the word "clever" mean? (Quick, resourceful, ingenious; using your head.) Look at the cover and talk about what this book might be about. Ask: Which one is Clever Beatrice? How does Beatrice look here? (Confident.) Discuss the giant. How does he look? (Confused, puzzled, unhappy.) Where do you think the story takes place? (In the woods, wilderness.) Are there really giants? Do you know what we call stories that are wild exaggerations, funny, and teach us something, too? (Tall tales.) **Let's read to find out** why Beatrice is clever.

WHILE READING: Read the first two pages. Ask: What do you think Beatrice is thinking? (She is thinking about which way she can best earn money for her mother; how she can outsmart the rich but stupid giant.) Read on. Note what Beatrice observes as she walks into the woods. After reading her first bet with the giant, ask for predictions about what she will do. Continue reading in this fashion throughout the three bets. Be sure to utilize the maps on the inside cover, especially when you get to the final bet! Beatrice's mother says she is "sharp as a tack." Discuss what this means.

FOLLOW-UP DISCUSSION: Ask: How does Beatrice's mother feel when she sees the bag of coins? At the end of the story the giant feels lucky. Why? Do you think he is lucky? Why? What does "clever" mean? Could this story really happen? Could someone really outsmart someone like the giant? Why? If you could be either rich or smart, which would you pick? Why? What do you like best about Beatrice? Would you like to have Beatrice as a friend? Discuss. Do you think the giant would like to have Beatrice as a friend? Make or trace an outline of Beatrice and enlarge. Use colorful yarn or heavy string to attach word cards generated by the children that list Beatrice's *character traits*. Trace outlines of the students. Cut them out and hang them around the room or along the hallway outside the classroom. Have each child attach word cards to her image listing her own character traits. Pretty clever!

For a listing of folk tales, legends, fairy tales, and fractured fairy tales, see Book Notes.

Text and illustrations copyright © 2001 CLEVER BEATRICE written by Margaret Wiley and illustrated by Heather S. Solomon. Used with permission of Atheneum Books for Young Readers, an imprint of Simon & Schuster Children's Publishing.

Notes:

Title	THE OTHER SIDE
Author	Jacqueline Woodson
Illustrator	E. B. Lewis
Publisher	Putnam
Copyright Date	2001
Ages	6 and up
Read-Aloud Time	7–8 minutes
Subject	Fences, friendship, differences; race; prejudice

In this quietly powerful story, Clover and Annie meet and become friends atop the fence that separates their properties and stretches through town. "Don't climb over that fence," warns Clover's mama. Clover's warned not to go on the other side. Annie's mama told her the same thing. "But she never said nothing about sitting on it." And so the girls sit on the fence and gradually bring their worlds a little closer together.

> **PREREADING FOCUS:** Ask: What is the purpose of a fence? Discuss. Show the cover of the book. Read the title. What do you think "the other side" is? What do you think this story might be about? Who are the *characters*? Who do you think will tell this story? (Girl in the foreground.) Why? Where do you think this story takes place? (Country; farm.) Why? (Open land, farm buildings in background.) What time of year do you think it is? (Summer.) Why? (Foliage, flowers.) **Let's read to find out** what the title means.

> **WHILE READING:** Read the first page. Ask: What time of year is it? Which girl on the cover is telling the story? (African-American girl.) Where does she live? (In the yellow house.) Why do you think her mother tells her it isn't safe to climb over the fence? Read through next two spreads. Ask: How do you think the girl on the fence feels when Sandra says she can't play with them? Why do you think Sandra does that? Annie doesn't say anything when Sandra snubs the girl on the fence. Why doesn't she? What would you have done if you were standing there when Sandra acted that way? What would you have said to the girl if she asked you? Discuss. Read on through the girls' meeting at the fence. Ask: Why does Annie like to sit on the fence? (She can see all over.) Have you ever sat on a fence? What was it like? How do you know that Clover wants to sit on the fence with Annie? How does Annie convince her that it's okay to sit on the fence? Read the next page. What do you think they're talking about on the fence? Why do you think Sandra is looking at them funny? Read to the end of the story.

> **FOLLOW-UP DISCUSSION:** Ask: What does the title mean? What do you think Annie wishes? (The fence would come down.) Why? Who else do you think feels that way? Annie and Clover became friends on the fence. How does Annie feel about that? (Good.) How do you know? (She stays up on the fence even though

Sandra stares at her.) How does Clover's mama feel about that? (Good.) How do you know? (She smiles and nods when she and Clover discuss it. She doesn't ask Clover to get down off the fence.) How are Annie and Clover different? How are they alike? How are you like your friends? How are you different? What makes a good friend? List traits on chart paper.

A light yet worthwhile read about being friends despite differences (this time in interests) is BEING FRIENDS, written by Karen Beaumont and illustrated by Joy Allen (Dial), for which a read-aloud plan can be found in the Pre-K–K volume of this series. For a humorous selection about friends, don't miss the "five stories about two great friends" in picture book format, entitled GEORGE AND MARTHA, by James Marshall (Houghton Mifflin).

For additional books about friendship, see Book Notes.

For an outstanding book that explores the subject of prejudice, see the read-aloud plan for MARTIN'S BIG WORDS: The Life of Martin Luther King, Jr., written by Doreen Rappaport, and illustrated by Bryan Collier (Hyperion).

Notes:

Title . . . . STUART'S CAPE
Author . . . . Sara Pennypacker
Illustrator . . . . Martin Matje
Publisher . . . . Orchard
Copyright Date 2002
Ages 6–8
Read-Aloud Time . . . . 6–8 minutes per chapter; 6 days
Subject . . . . Fantasy, adventure, imagination, the magical power of a CAPE!

Note: Find a cape to wear as you read a chapter from this book each day. Don't have one? Make one like Stuart's! Surely you or someone you know has 100 or so ties they no longer have a use for (or you'd like to suggest they no longer have a use for). And a stapler? No problem! You're an educator! Now the purple sock—that may pose more of a challenge . . . .

Stuart is new in town. He has no friends, the trash man instead of the movers picked up all his great junk, and he's a worry wart. What if there are man-eating spiders in his new closet? Or worse, a man, eating spiders? What if he can't find the bathroom in his new school and once he locates it, he gets locked inside and the firemen have to be called? What if no one wants to be his friend? As if worrying's not bad enough, it's raining and Stuart is bored. Until, that is, a bunch of old ties and a rumpled purple sock become a cape with the help of a rusty stapler. And then the adventures begin. One a day, different each day, like the chapters you'll read from this hilarious, heartwarming account of the misadventures of one sort-of everyday eight-year-old boy who loves toast and likes his bed toasty.

> **PREREADING FOCUS:** *Introducing the book:* Ask: Who has a cape they like to wear? What does it look like? Why are capes fun to wear? What do you do when you wear your cape? What do you feel like when you wear your cape? (A hero!) What happens to heroes? (They have adventures!) Don your cape with a flourish and begin reading!

> **WHILE READING:** Read a chapter a day. This book has a wonderful circular plan in which something from the previous chapter/adventure finds its way into the next chapter. The segues are fabulous! Each day before you begin, recap briefly what happened in the previous chapter so that you can maximize the pleasure and laughs from Stuart's next misadventure!

*Note preparation for Day 3.

Day One: "Stuart Makes a Cape"

>**Follow-up**: Have a volunteer dramatize Stuart's actions in his cape (pp. 6–7). Ask: Who do you think is at the door? Ask children to bring in things from home to make their own capes, or consider making a classroom cape. Ask children to collect and bring in old ties (and a purple sock) from home. Make a STUART CAPE!

Illustration from STUART'S CAPE copyright © 2000 by Martin Matje, used by permission of Orchard Books/Scholastic Inc.

Day Two: Chapter 1, "Playing Stuart"

Prereading: Ask: What do we know about Stuart? (He has just moved to Punbury. He worries a lot. He's good at it. He has no friends.) What kind of day is Stuart having? (He is bored. It's raining. He doesn't have anyone to play with.) What is Stuart worrying about? (School starts in a few days, man-eating spiders, a man eating spiders hiding in his closet, the school bathroom, no friends.) What was Stuart doing before he decided to make a cape? (Playing dinosaurs, horses, and gorillas.) Why did he decide to make a cape? (So he could have an adventure.) What other characters did we meet? (One-Tooth, Stuart's cat; Aunt Bubbles; his mother; his father.) What happened to all of Stuart's best stuff? (The trash collector instead of the movers took it.) How did Stuart make his cape? (With 100 ties, a purple sock, and a rusty stapler.) **Let's read to find out** who is at the door.

Follow-up: Ask: Why didn't Stuart act surprised when he answered the door? (He knows that people who wear capes never act surprised.) How did One-Tooth react? (Scared.) What complaint do the visiting animals have? (Stuart's playing animals all wrong, and it's rude to play animals.) What do the animals say they do all day? (Eat, sleep, stand.) What happens when the animals play Stuart? (They wake up, they get dressed, they get cleaned up, they play hide-and-seek, and they eat.) What does Stuart eat? (An entire angel food cake.) Have you ever eaten angel food cake? What does it taste like? (Make the point that angel food cake is light and airy.) What do Stuart's parents do throughout the chapter? (They yell for him to quiet down.) Why doesn't Stuart think he'll be getting bored again? (He has a cape!) Begin work on capes.

Day Three: Chapter 2, "Stuart Flies"

Note: Consider serving angel food cake and pound cake following the reading of this chapter so children can compare the two.

Prereading: Read the chapter title. Ask: What do you think will happen in this chapter? (Stuart will fly!) What do you think his mother and father will do? **Let's read to find out** what happens in Stuart's flying adventure.

Follow-up: Ask: How does Stuart react when he wakes up and realizes that he can fly? (He remembers not to act surprised. "Good," he says.) What do Stuart's parents and Aunt Bubbles say? (Hush! Quiet! Shhhh!) How does Stuart keep himself down? (With tape.) What does the air feel like as Stuart flies around? (As soft and cool as whipped cream.) What do the houses look like? (Chocolate chips in a little cookie town.) What does Stuart worry about? (Robbers, wolves, snakes, no friends, getting down.) How does Stuart figure out how to get down? (When Aunt Bubbles mentions the missing angel food cake being lighter than air, he asks her to go to the store for a *heavy* pound cake.) How does Aunt Bubbles get the pound cake to Stuart? (She makes a slingshot from a tire on the car.) Sample angel food and pound cakes and discuss their textures. Continue working on capes.

Day Four: Chapter 3, "Stuart Grows Toast"

Prereading: Read the chapter title. Ask: Can you grow toast? Why not? Do you like toast? Why? (List answers on chart paper.) **Let's read to find out** how Stuart grows toast!

Follow-up: Ask: How does Stuart grow toast? (He plants the seeds he finds in his cape pocket and waters them with melted butter.) What does he worry about while the toast is growing? (What if his 5's come out backward? What if he's the shortest kid in the class? No friends.) What is Stuart's best thing? (Worrying.) What is his worst thing? (Waiting.) What was the bad thing about the neighbors? (None were going into third grade.) What was the best thing? (None of them were robbers, and none had seen any wolves or snakes in the neighborhood.) Why does the leftover toast make a good bed? (It's warm!) Ask: What's your best thing? What's your worst thing? Make a chart listing one-word answers across from each child's name in "Best" and "Worst" columns. Use a different color for each column. Keep working on those you-know-whats!

Day Five: Chapter 4, "A Bad Start"

Prereading: Ask: What was Stuart about to do as we left him? (Get in his warm bed.) What do you think his bad start might be? **Let's read to find out** about Stuart's bad start.

Follow-up: Ask: What is an orientation day? (New students can visit the school a day early. It's a practice day.) How does Stuart feel about going? (Terrible idea.) Why? (It's an extra first day. Twice as many things could go wrong.) The author of this book plants details in the story that later become important parts of the story. What are some of the things we learned in this chapter that might become important in the next chapter? (It's trash day. His cat likes to knock over trash cans. One-Tooth is sleeping on his cape.) Finish cape(s)!

Day Six: Chapter 5, "Trading Places"

Prereading: Review what happened in the last chapter. **Let's read to find out** why this chapter is titled "Trading Places." Have children wear their capes as you read or allow children to take turns wearing the class cape throughout the day.

Follow-up: Ask: What does the title mean? (One-Tooth and the trash man traded places.) How does Stanley help them trade back? (He puts them back in their right places.) What is Stanley's job, and what is his work? (Job—trash collector; work—collecting treasured junk.) What happens at the end of the book? (Stuart goes to school. He's late and everyone else has gone home, but he realizes he's made a friend.) Who is his new friend? (Stanley.)

For more about Stuart and his adventures, refer fans to the sequel, STUART GOES TO SCHOOL (Orchard).

Notes:

Title	DUMPY LA RUE
Author	Elizabeth Winthrop
Illustrator	Betsy Lewin
Publisher	Holt
Copyright Date	2001
Ages	5–8
Read-Aloud Time	6–8 minutes
Subject	Dance, following your heart, being true to yourself

Dumpy La Rue wants to dance. "You're a pig," say his father and mother. "Boys don't dance," says his sister. But Dumpy La Rue is a pig who knows what he wants to do. And this "porker with passion" is so convincing as he twirls, jetés, and flies through the air, that pretty soon he's got the entire farmyard tapping their hooves, wanting to join in. No music? No problem! Dumpy advises, "If you want to dance, if you want to glide, just close your eyes and listen inside." In twos and threes the barnyard bunch shimmy, curl, two-step, and shuffle. Even Dumpy's persnickety sister bounces a little "on the sly" at the barnyard ballet.

PREREADING FOCUS: Before showing the book to listeners, ask: Have you ever wanted to do something so badly, even though everyone told you that you couldn't or shouldn't or wouldn't be able to do it, that you tried anyway? What happened? Discuss. Today we're going to read a story about a barnyard animal that wants to dance. Now what barnyard animal do you think would be the worst at dancing? Elicit answers. The barnyard animal in this story that wants to dance is called Dumpy La Rue. What kind of barnyard animal might have that name? When you think of "dumpy," what comes to mind? Show the cover of the book revealing that Dumpy La Rue is a pig. **Let's read to find out** more about Dumpy La Rue.

WHILE READING: Read with expression. The comments from mother, father, and especially sister, beg for big drama contrasted with the dreamy, wistful description of Dumpy's dancing escapades. Emphasize the verb play in this rhythmic, rhyming text as you—and the barnyard pals—cavort across the pages.

FOLLOW-UP DISCUSSION: Ask: Who can remember a word from the story that was used to describe one of the barnyard animals as he danced? Ask for volunteers to demonstrate these vivid verbs! You've got shimmied, curled, two-step, shuffle, salsa, glide, glissade, bourrée, jeté, slip, slide, twirl, raising a snout to the sky, and spreading hooves far and wide pretending to fly! Have fun!

For other books on the subject of dance, both serious and silly, see DEGAS AND THE DANCE, written by Susan Goldman Rubin (Abrams); DANCE!, by Elisha Cooper (Greenwillow); ALICIA'S TUTU, written by Robin Pulver and illustrated by Mark Graham (Dial); NUTCRACKER NOEL, written by Kate McMullan and illustrated by Jim McMullan (HarperCollins); and ANGELINA BALLERINA, written by Katharine Holabird and illustrated by Helen Craig (Pleasant Company).

For another book about a character who knew what he wanted to do, reach for the black-and-white classic about a gentle-hearted bull, THE STORY OF FERDINAND, written by Munro Leaf and illustrated by Robert Lawson (Viking) and first published in 1936. One more title to consider is DAHLIA, by Barbara McClintock (Farrar, Straus & Giroux), about a girl who gets a doll she doesn't want and another surprise from her Aunt Edme.

*Cover of DUMPY LA RUE, copyright 2001 by Betsy Lewin,
used with permission of Henry Holt and Company.*

Notes:

Title	PUNCTUATION TAKES A VACATION
Author	Robin Pulver
Illustrator	Lynn Rowe Reed
Publisher	Holiday House
Copyright Date	2003
Ages	6–8
Read-Aloud Time	6–8 minutes
Subject . . . . . the importance and purpose of various punctuation marks

Note: For follow-up activity, have ready postcards or postcard-sized tagboard for each child. Copy simple punctuation rules from the book on colorful poster board or chart paper to display in the classroom. Once children have completed their postcards, arrange them jauntily around the list of rules.

What would writing be like without punctuation? Day after day punctuation marks do their work, only to be scoffed at, ignored, corrected, and insulted. Teachers work and work to get students to embrace the curly commas, the talkative quotation marks, the emotional exclamation marks. But when they won't take possession (as an apostrophe would), it's time for a punctuation vacation. At first the class cheers, but gradually they realize just what a big problem it is if *theyre expected to write without the help of periods commas apostrophes colons quotation marks and exclamation points help they yell but no ones around to offer relief theyre all on vacation at Take-a-Break Lake sunning themselves from 1000AM until swim time at 300 sharp.* (There. Now wasn't that hard to read without punctuation?)

> **PREREADING FOCUS:** Ask: What is punctuation? (Marks used when writing to make thoughts clear to reader.) What are some examples of punctuation we use? (Periods, commas, apostrophes, colons, exclamation points, and question marks.) Why do we use punctuation? (To help the reader understand what we are writing.) What would happen if we didn't use punctuation? (It would be hard to understand the meaning of written words.) **Let's read to find out** what happens when punctuation takes a vacation. Show the cover of the book. Identify the different types of punctuation shown in the windows of the plane.

> **WHILE READING:** Read the first two spreads. Ask: Why do you think Mr. Wright wants to give punctuation a vacation? (Hard to teach; he's exasperated.) Read on through Mr. Wright's read-aloud session. Show the page. Ask: What do you think will happen now? Read on. As you read the postcards from the punctuation marks, point out what the message is! Guess which punctuation mark has written each card. After reading their letter to the punctuation marks, pass the book around to show the children the page. Ask: What's wrong here? (The punctuation is all messed up!) Read to the end.

FOLLOW-UP DISCUSSION: Ask: What happened when the punctuation returned? Review the rules at the end of the book. Have children choose one punctuation mark and write a postcard from that mark to its friends at Take-a-Break Lake telling them how it felt to be back from vacation. Children must use that punctuation mark as much as possible. Follow the style of the postcards in the book. Display postcards and punctuation rules.

A wonderful accompaniment to this book, one that ought not to be missed, is THE AMAZING POP-UP GRAMMAR BOOK, by Jennie Maizels and Kate Petty (Dutton), which truly lives up to its name! Whoever said it's impossible to make grammar fun?!?

For books about writing letters and other correspondence, see the read-aloud plans for DEAR MRS. LARUE LETTERS FROM OBEDIENCE SCHOOL, by Mark Teague (Scholastic) and CLICK, CLACK, MOO COWS THAT TYPE, written by Doreen Cronin and illustrated by Betsy Lewin (Simon & Schuster), found elsewhere in this part of this book. Consult Tips and Techniques for Teachers and Librarians and Book Notes for more writing-related titles.

Notes:

Title	MARTIN'S BIG WORDS: The Life of Martin Luther King, Jr.
Author	Doreen Rappaport
Illustrator	Bryan Collier
Publisher	Hyperion
Copyright Date	2001
Ages	6–8
Read-Aloud Time	5–7 minutes
Subject	Simple biography of the life of Dr. Martin Luther King Jr.

Note: In preparation for follow-up activity, print quotations found in this book on the bottom of drawing paper or on placards to be placed below children's drawings of Martin's big words for display in the classroom.

"You are as good as anyone," proclaim the words on the first page of this magnificent book full of the big words of a giant among men. Memorable, thought-provoking quotations weave through a simple biography accompanied by compelling art to make a book that has garnered a number of prestigious awards, including a Caldecott Honor, the Coretta Scott King Award, and a Best Illustrated Children's Book from the *New York Times Review*. Pared and honed to aching simplicity, King's assassination is explained with just ten words: "On his second day there, he was shot. He died." MARTIN'S BIG WORDS is big, keeping Martin Luther's King Jr.'s spirit alive and accessible to the youngest of listeners and readers.

> **PREREADING FOCUS:** Show the cover of the book. Ask: Does anyone recognize this man? (MLK.) What can you tell me about him? Turn to the back cover and read the title. What are "big words"? What do we call a book about a person's life? (A biography.) **Let's read to find out** about the life of Martin Luther King Jr.

> **WHILE READING:** Read the first page of text. Why would his mother's words make Martin feel better? After reading the next page, ask: Why would Martin's father's words make him feel good? Read the third page of text. The author calls Martin's words, big words (Repeat the quotation on this page.), but these words are simple. Why do you think he calls them big? (Big message, big meaning.) Read through the explanation of Rosa Parks and the bus boycotts. Ask: Why did the city leaders finally agree that black citizens could sit anywhere they wanted? Read the next two pages. Ask: What are equal rights? Read the next several pages. Ask: What did Martin believe was the way to make change? (Peaceful protests: love, marches, singing, praying together, sharing dreams.) Read to the end.

> **FOLLOW-UP DISCUSSION:** Ask: How long did it take for MLK's peaceful protests to end segregation in the South? (10 years.) Why did MLK win the Nobel Peace Prize? (He taught others to fight with words, not fists.) Why was MLK in Memphis on the day he was shot? (He went to help garbage collectors on strike.)

Ask: Why do you think the author gave this book this title? Pass out quotations and ask children to illustrate Martin's big words. Display.

Other notable picture books on the subject of Martin Luther King Jr. include HAPPY BIRTHDAY, MARTIN LUTHER KING, written by Jean Marzollo and illustrated by Brian Pinkney (Scholastic) and A PICTURE BOOK OF MARTIN LUTHER KING, JR., written by by David Adler and illustrated by Robert Casilla (Holiday House). Additional books and Web sites are listed in the back of MARTIN'S BIG WORDS.

Also, see A BUS OF OUR OWN, written by Freddi Williams Evans and illustrated by Shawn Costello (Whitman), for a story based on real events about a community that, in the pre-civil rights era, works together to get a bus to take their African-American children to school.

Cover of MARTIN'S BIG WORDS: THE LIFE OF MARTIN LUTHER KING, JR., copyright 2001 by Bryan Collier, reprinted with permission of Hyperion Books for Children.

Notes:

Title	OFFICER BUCKLE AND GLORIA
Author/Illustrator	Peggy Rathmann
Publisher	Putnam
Copyright Date	1995
Ages	5 and up
Read-Aloud Time	8–10 minutes
Subject	Safety rules, dogs, humor

Note: Prepare large, star-shaped pieces of colorful paper on which to write safety tips, mentioned by Officer Buckle and dramatized by Gloria, following the reading of this story.

Hands down, this is my favorite Rathmann book. That's not to say I don't love reading about the fate of Bootsie Barker who bites, or saying Good Night to that adorable gorilla, but there's something about Gloria that makes her my standout favorite among this author's characters. And the fact that listeners come away with an appreciation of simple but serious safety rules makes this Caldecott Medal winner a must-have.

PREREADING FOCUS: Show the cover of the book. Read the title. Ask: Who is Officer Buckle? (Policeman.) Who is Gloria? (Dog.) Where do you think this story takes place, or what is the *setting*? (School auditorium.) How does Gloria look? How does Officer Buckle look? How do the children look? What do you think Officer Buckle might be talking about with the children? **Let's read to find out**.

WHILE READING: Read through the book. Take time to explore and enjoy the illustrations, which tell much more than the words! Before Gloria joins Officer Buckle, ask why the children fall asleep and snore. (They are bored.) On the page of letters Officer Buckle receives from the children, note that the letters are addressed to *Gloria* and Officer Buckle. Ask why. Read the myriad safety tips found throughout the book.

FOLLOW-UP DISCUSSION: Review the safety tips Officer Buckle and Gloria taught in the schools they visited. Discuss each one and place it on star-shaped paper. Ask: Can you think of others? Have children illustrate the tips and display them around the room.

For another comical look at safety—this time while riding a bicycle—see the read-aloud plan for BEAR'S BICYCLE, written by Emilie Warren McLeod and illustrated by David McPhail (Little, Brown), found elsewhere in this part of this book.

See Book Notes and the subject index for other books about dogs.

Notes:

Title	MISS SMITH'S INCREDIBLE STORYBOOK
Author/Illustrator	Michael Garland
Publisher	Dutton
Copyright Date	2003
Ages	5 and up
Read-Aloud Time	8–10 minutes
Subject	Fairy tale characters, the magic of reading, magical teachers

Note: This book makes for an excellent introduction to a school year that will be filled with memorable story times. It also offers a creative introduction to a unit on the study of fairy tales and fractured fairy tales.

From the moment Miss Smith walks into her second grade classroom on the first day of school, Zack senses something is different. And from her very first story time, he knows he's right. Storybook characters come to life and the classroom transforms into a pirate ship. Zack can even feel "the breeze in his hair and hear the waves pounding on the side of the ship." With outstanding illustrations, Garland leads us through a story that becomes more fantastic with each page. In Miss Smith's absence, fairy-tale characters create such chaos that Principal Rittenrotten calls in a team of firefighters. But Miss Smith comes to the rescue with a look and a book, and in the end, the message is loud and clear: "Who would have guessed that reading could be so much fun?"

PREREADING FOCUS: Ask: Do you like to hear stories read aloud? Why? Show the cover of the book and read the title. Ask children to identify Miss Smith. Ask why there are kids surrounding her. How do they look? Discuss who the characters might be. **Let's read to find out** why these characters are gathered around Miss Smith.

WHILE READING: Read the first spread. Ask: What would you think if Miss Smith were your new teacher? What is she holding? Read the next two spreads. Ask: Have you ever felt as if you were part of a story—right in the book—when someone was reading a story to you? Read the next spread. Ask: What story is Miss Smith reading? (Red Riding Hood.) Read through the next several spreads. Note storybook characters as they appear and discuss who they are and which stories they are from. Ask: Why does Zack think they ought to finish the stories? (Because every time Miss Smith finishes a story, the characters whoosh back into the book.) Spend some time identifying the characters in, on, and around the school on the spread in which Miss Smith races to the rescue and on the tug-of-war spread. Enjoy the next spread! (Try perfecting THAT look!) Read to the end of the story. On the last page, note the character that didn't whoosh back into the book!

FOLLOW-UP DISCUSSION: Ask: Which fairy-tale characters are your favorites? List them and ask children to briefly tell the story. Launch a study of fractured fairy tales. See Book Notes for book suggestions.

For a creatively packaged, absorbing, and humorous follow-up, read WHO'S AFRAID OF THE BIG BAD BOOK?, by Lauren Child (Hyperion), in which Herb falls asleep on his book—or rather falls into his book—and the adventure begins.

For a lighthearted follow-up read-aloud, consider GOLDIE LOCKS HAS CHICKEN POX, written by Erin Dealey and illustrated by Hanako Wakiyama (Atheneum), in which storybook and nursery rhyme characters visit Goldie Locks and her terrible-teaser-of-a-brother as she recuperates from chicken pox. Another fine choice is STELLA LOUELLA'S RUNAWAY BOOK, by Lisa Campbell Ernst (Simon & Schuster), in which an array of characters who have read and passed along Louella's missing library book join in her search to recover it. Gather the clues from their favorite parts to discover which much-loved tale the book is about. Finally, don't miss EACH PEACH PEAR PLUM, by Janet and Allan Ahlberg (Puffin), for which a read-aloud plan can be found in the Pre-K–K volume of this series.

For a book of poetry that celebrates reading, get a copy of GOOD BOOKS, GOOD TIMES!, poems selected by Lee Bennett Hopkins and illustrated by Harvey Stevenson (HarperCollins).

For additional fairy-tale selections, refer to Book Notes.

Notes:

Title	STAND TALL, MOLLY LOU MELON
Author	Patty Lovell
Illustrator	David Catrow
Publisher	Putnam
Copyright Date	2001
Ages	5–up
Read-Aloud Time	8–10 minutes
Subject	Bullies, believing in yourself, wise advice, grandparents

Molly Lou Melon is the shortest girl in first grade. But her grandmother tells her, "Walk as proudly as you can and the world will look up to you." So she does. She follows her grandmother's advice for all the bumps in life, even when she moves and starts in a new school where Ronald Durkin lurks. He works hard to make Molly miserable, but instead, Molly succeeds in making him kinder. Grandma was right. Pass it on.

PREREADING FOCUS: Ask: What is a bully? How does a bully make you feel? How should we react to a bully? **Let's read to find out** how Molly Lou Melon responds to a bully.

WHILE READING: Read through the first several spreads, noting the details in Molly Lou Melon's world. Enjoy the artist's perspective. Build upon the structure of the text while reading aloud. ("So she did.") As you read through the second half of the book, ask: Why do you think Ronald Durkin is picking on Molly? (Because she is new to the school; she is little; she is different.) Why do you think Molly Lou Melon seems not to be bothered by Ronald Durkin? (Self-confidence.) How many days does it take for Molly Lou Melon to win over Ronald Durkin? (Five.)

FOLLOW-UP DISCUSSION: Review the things that Grandma taught Molly Lou Melon. Write them on chart paper. "Walk as proudly as you can and the world will look up to you. Smile big and the world will smile right alongside you. Sing out clear and strong and the world will cry tears of joy. Believe in yourself and the world will believe in you too." Have children copy their favorite on a tagboard strip and decorate with lots of little details in the style of the artwork of the book.

For other books on the subject of bullies, see the read-aloud plan for COCK-A-DOODLE DUDLEY, by Bill Peet (Houghton Mifflin). See also TYRONE THE HORRIBLE and TYRONE THE DOUBLE DIRTY ROTTEN CHEATER, by Hans Wilhelm (Scholastic); and THE RECESS QUEEN, written by Alexis O'Neill and illustrated by Laura Huliska-Beith (Scholastic). More titles are listed in Book Notes.

See the read-aloud plan found elsewhere in this book for AMAZING GRACE, written by Mary Hoffman and illustrated by Caroline Binch (Dial), another book about the power of a strong relationship between a child and her wise, supportive grandmother.

Notes:

Title	THE HALLO-WIENER
Author/Illustrator	Dav Pilkey
Publisher	Scholastic
Copyright Date	1995
Ages	5 and up
Read-Aloud Time	6–8 minutes
Subject	Halloween night, bullies, self-reliance, resourcefulness, friendship

Oscar is half-a-dog tall and one-and-a-half dogs long. All the other dogs make fun of him, until on Halloween night he saves them from the graveyard monster—two cats in a costume that only Oscar can discern because of his size. Long before this author/illustrator made underpants more than just underwear (CAPTAIN UNDERPANTS) came this light and comic holiday tale with lines sure to hit the funny bone of adults as well as children. There are lines such as this one when Oscar shows up in his wiener costume: "Oscar showed up looking quite frank," and when the neighborhood gang goes trick-or-treating: "All night long the other dogs hounded every treat they could get their paws on." Find out how Oscar goes from being "Wiener Dog" to "Hero Sandwich" on one gently spooky, mighty hilarious night.

PREREADING FOCUS: Look at the cover. Ask the children what they think this story is about. Note the other dogs making fun of Oscar. Ask: Who do you think is the main character? (When they point to Oscar, name him.) Why? (In the middle.) Discuss how Oscar looks. (Unhappy.) When the children notice the hot dog, ask: Why do you think there is a hot dog on the cover? Tell children that Oscar is a dachshund, which is often nicknamed a "wiener" dog. Ask for other names for a wiener. (Hot dog, frank, frankfurter.) Does anyone have a dachshund as a pet? If so, ask what it is like. Read the title of the book. Ask: At what time of year do you think this story takes place? (Fall; Halloween.) **Let's read to find out** why all the other dogs are laughing at Oscar.

WHILE READING: Read the first four spreads. Ask: What do you think Oscar will be for Halloween? Read on through trick-or-treating. Ask: How is Oscar feeling? (Sad.) Why? (Friends are making fun of him; he doesn't like his costume; no treats.) Read to the page where the cats are visible through their monster costume. Ask: What does Oscar see that the others did not see? (Cat's tail.) Why did he see it? (His size.) Read to the end of the story.

FOLLOW-UP DISCUSSION: In the end of the story, what does Oscar do to show he is a true friend? (Exposes the cats; doesn't make fun of the other dogs; offers the dogs a ride back to shore.)

For additional selections on the subject of Halloween, see Book Notes.

For more books on the fall season, don't miss the rhythmical, toe-tapping BARN DANCE!, written by Bill Martin Jr. and John Archambault and illustrated by Ted Rand (Holt).

From THE HALLO-WIENER by Dav Pilkey. Published by the Blue Sky Press/Scholastic Inc. Copyright © 1995 by Dav Pilkey.

Notes:

Title. . . . . DEAR MRS. LARUE: LETTERS FROM OBEDIENCE SCHOOL	
Author/Illustrator . . . . Mark Teague	
Publisher. . . . . Scholastic	
Copyright Date 2002	
Ages. 6–9	
Read-Aloud Time. . . . . 8–10 minutes	
Subject . . . . Writing letters, dogs, obedience school, inferences	

"Dear Anyone Who Will Listen," starts the letter from Ike LaRue to readers on the flap of the jacket. Read that letter and you'll be hooked. You'll just have to turn the page to find out what happens to the "loyal and misunderstood" pip of a pup that's stuck in the Igor Brotweiler Canine Academy for BAD DOGS.

On each spread inside you'll find gloomy, black-and-white pictures of how Ike is painting his stay, contrasted with bright, bold, inviting glimpses of the academy as it really is. And on each page you'll be treated to the hilarious letters Ike sends daily to his mistress entreating her to reconsider his incarceration. Laughs galore. Letters that get the message across. A classic picture book to be sure. Don't miss this one!

PREREADING FOCUS: Show the magnificent cover of this big book. Read the title. Note and discuss details. Ask: What is "obedience school"? (A place where animals—usually dogs—learn to follow commands.) What other words come from the word *obedience*? (Obey, disobey, obedient.) What do they mean? Ask for predictions of what this story might be about. **Let's read to find out** why this dog is writing a letter.

WHILE READING: Read the first spread. Note the date of the news article. Ask: How would you describe Ike? (He misbehaves!) Review what has been learned from the news article. Turn the page and the fun begins! Point out the contrast between the black-and-white picture on the right and the color illustration on the left. Note the details. Read the letter. Discuss. Elicit inferences from children. Read the letter of October 2. Enjoy the spread. Discuss the facts that led to Ike being taken to obedience school. Read the next page. Ask: What do you think *melodramatic* means? Read the letter of October 4. Note Mrs. La Rue's bad habit. Note discrepancies in letter and color illustration. Contrast illustrations. Continue through the escape. Ask: What do you think will happen next? Read the October 10 news article. Note the use of the word *melodramatic*. Read through to the rescue. Don't miss Ike's rolling skills! Read the last two pages. Note what that rapscallion is doing on the last page! (Eating chicken pie!)

FOLLOW-UP DISCUSSION: Ask: What do you think Mrs. LaRue will say when she sees Ike? Did you enjoy Ike's letters? Why? Read the back flap of the jacket, on which Teague tells about the inspiration for this book. Have students write a letter from their pet to them about something they did that they weren't supposed to do. Have them illustrate the letter with a picture of their pip of a pet. Display the letters.

For other excellent books that celebrate writing in creative and memorable ways, see the read-aloud plans found elsewhere in this book for CLICK, CLACK, MOO: COWS THAT TYPE, written by Doreen Cronin and illustrated by Betsy Lewin (Simon & Schuster), and PUNCUATION TAKES A VACATION, written by Robin Pulver and illustrated by Lynn Rowe Reed (Holiday House).

For additional titles, see Book Notes and Tips and Techniques for Teachers and Librarians.

From DEAR MRS. LARUE by Mark Teague. Published by Scholastic Press/Scholastic Inc. © 2002 by Mark Teague. Used by permission.

Notes:

Title . . . . THE ROUGH-FACE GIRL	
Author . . . . Rafe Martin	
Illustrator . . . . David Shannon	
Publisher . . . . Putnam	
Copyright Date 1992	
Ages 7–9	
Read-Aloud Time . . . . 8–10 minutes	
Subject . . . . Algonquin Indian version of Cinderella, justice, Native American culture	

Note: This book is a valuable addition to a collection of alternative versions of classic fairy tales.

My daughter's favorite fairy tale since she was old enough to point to the book she wanted to hear has been "Cinderella." Her collection of variations on this most classic of tales fills a wide shelf. From pop-up board books to Disney renditions to a lushly illustrated retelling of the original, these books hold a special place beside her bed. I'm convinced it's the theme: She has always been deeply affected by issues of fairness and justice. Of all these versions of the fairy tale "Cinderella," this one holds a special place for its beautiful language from author Rafe Martin and its striking illustrations by the popular David Shannon of NO, DAVID! fame. Published first in 1992, this book has garnered prestigious awards such as the IRA Teachers' Choice Book, ABC Children's Booksellers' Choice, and numerous state awards.

PREREADING FOCUS: Show the cover of the book and read the title. Ask children what they can tell about this character from the cover. (Native American; embarrassed or self-conscious of face; skin covered with bandages.) **Let's read to find out** what fairy tale this Algonquin Indian tale reminds us of.

WHILE READING: Read the first page. If this story is part of a unit on Native American studies, find the location of this tribe on a map. Read through the story, noting the cultural references in text and illustrations. After reading the page on which the Rough-Face girl sees the face of the Invisible Being, ask: What is the Invisible Being? (Nature.) When the Rough-Face Girls meets the Invisible Being's sister, ask: Why is the Invisible Being's sister called wise? ("When she looked at you she would look you right in the eyes and she could see all the way down to your heart.") What did she see when she looked at the Rough-Face Girl? (A beautiful, kind heart.)

FOLLOW-UP DISCUSSION: Near the end of the story, it says, "Now anyone could see that she was, indeed, beautiful. But the Invisible Being and his sister had seen that from the start." Discuss what this means. Ask: Why do you think the Invisible Being is happy to marry the Rough-Face Girl? What qualities does the

Rough-Face Girl possess? (Faith in herself; courage; a kind heart.) What fairy tale does this story remind you of? (Cinderella.) List similarities. What do you like about this version of the tale? Do you like it as much as other versions you have heard or read? Compare and contrast.

For a rib-tickling, turned-on-its-ear version of Cinderella with a meaty message, don't miss BIGFOOT CINDERRRRRELLA, written by Tony Johnston and illustrated by James Warhola (Putnam), in which Cinderella is a member of a "band of Bigfoots" and a grizzly is her "beary godfather."

Additional fairy-tale, tall-tale, and fractured fairy-tale titles are listed in Book Notes.

Notes:

Title	ZELDA AND IVY: THREE STORIES ABOUT THE FABULOUS FOX SISTERS
Author/Illustrator	Laura McGee Kvasnosky
Publisher	Candlewick
Copyright Date	1998
Ages	6–8
Read-Aloud Time	8–10 minutes
Subject	Siblings: the pros and cons

Zelda is older; Ivy is younger. In the three chapters of this Oppenheim Toy Portfolio Gold Seal Award winner and School Library Journal Best Book of the Year, we learn how Zelda teases, torments, and takes care of her sister as the spirit moves her and the situation warrants. Follow the girls as they perform a circus act, jazz up their tails, and make wishes in short and satisfying chapters that end with things as they truly are between siblings.

PREREADING FOCUS: Show the cover of the book. Note details. Tell listeners that Zelda and Ivy are sisters. Zelda is the older sister. Ask children which character they think is which. **Let's read to find out** what happens as Zelda and Ivy play together throughout the day.

WHILE READING: As you complete each chapter, note what happens to Ivy at Zelda's hands. Discuss. Ask children how they think Ivy feels as she falls off the swing, has her tail primped, and gets the baton she covets. Ask children if they would have done what Ivy did in each chapter or if they would have behaved differently. Discuss. When Ivy looks for Zelda's baton in the last chapter, ask children what she has realized. (Zelda has given her baton to her sister.) How do you think Ivy feels? How does Zelda feel when Ivy offers to share?

FOLLOW-UP DISCUSSION: Ask: What do you think the girls will do next? Discuss sibling play. Ask: Are you the older sister or brother, the younger, both, or neither? What's good about being oldest, youngest, or only? Do you like to play with your brothers or sisters? Why? Is it different than playing with friends? How? Why? Are you more like Zelda or Ivy? Discuss. Which character do you like better? Why?

For more about Zelda and Ivy, see ZELDA AND IVY AND THE BOY NEXT DOOR and ZELDA AND IVY ONE CHRISTMAS (Candlewick). For Zelda and Ivy activities, visit the author's Web site: www.LMKbooks.com.

For a delightful treatment of family and feelings with tons of humor, see SPINKY SULKS, by William Steig (Farrar, Straus & Giroux).

For additional titles about family, refer to Book Notes.

ZELDA & IVY © 1998 by Laura McGee Kvasnosky. Reproduced by permission of the publisher Candlewick Press, Inc., Cambridge, MA.

Notes:

Title	THANKSGIVING AT THE TAPPLETONS'
Author	Eileen Spinelli
Illustrator	Maryann Cocca-Leffler
Publisher	Addison-Wesley; HarperCollins
Copyright Date	1982
Ages	4–8
Read-Aloud Time	6–8 minutes
Subject	Thanksgiving, family, reunions, values, what matters most

Note: See follow-up discussion for preparation of a sampling of the Tappletons' Thanksgiving meal.

Since I discovered this book in the early 1990s in a small, independent bookstore in Happy Valley, the home of Penn State University, it has remained my favorite picture book about the all-American holiday that brings family together. I love the Tappletons, and I'd like to have dinner with them any time, anywhere—even though I'm not partial to liverwurst.

From before dawn when Mrs. Tappleton lights the oven for the turkey, things go awry. How the Thanksgiving dinner that wasn't manages to satisfy Grandfather's growing hunger and Uncle Fritz's rumbling stomach will be certain to delight your audience with humor, warmth, and creative problem solving.

PREREADING FOCUS: Begin by discussing family traditions for Thanksgiving. Talk about traditional foods, the season, their favorite parts of the holiday. Show the cover of the book and read the title. Ask: What are these people doing? (Getting ready for Thanksgiving meal.) What is the centerpiece called? (A cornucopia.) What is it filled with? (Fruit.) Why do you think this is a common centerpiece at this time of year? (Harvest.) **Let's read to find out** about Thanksgiving at the Tappletons'.

WHILE READING: As you read through the occurrences that add up to a dismaying beginning to the Thanksgiving meal, note the details in the illustrations. As the story unfolds, ask children what they think will happen when everyone sits down to eat and there is no turkey, no potatoes, no salad, and no pies. Use expression as you read about Uncle Fritz and his stomach and Grandfather and the increasing number of elephants! After you read Grandmother's wise prayer of Thanksgiving, ask children what else could have happened instead. (Everyone could have complained, gotten angry, cried, grumbled, roared.) Read on to find out how they turn their dinner fiasco into a cherished family memory.

FOLLOW-UP DISCUSSION: Ask: Why didn't it matter to the Tappletons what they had to eat after all? (What mattered most was that they were together.) If you were at the Tappletons' Thanksgiving dinner table and had to think of something to eat, what would you have suggested? What would you have liked that the Tappletons served? Daring? Sample liverwurst and cheese sandwiches, pickles, and applesauce! Yum, yum!

See also THE MEMORY CUPBOARD: A THANKSGIVING STORY, written by Charlotte Herman and illustrated by Ben F. Stahl (Whitman), in which Katie learns that it is people, not things, that make memories.

See Book Notes for additional holiday and family titles.

Notes:

Title . . . . THE BORROWED HANUKKAH LATKES	
Author . . . . Linda Glaser	
Illustrator . . . . Nancy Cote	
Publisher . . . . Whitman	
Copyright Date 1997	
Ages 5–8	
Read-Aloud Time . . . . 6–8 minutes	
Subject . . . . Neighbors, Hanukkah, caring about others	

Note: Use the recipe found at the beginning of the book to prepare a batch of latkes for the class to enjoy following the reading of this book. For even more fun, make them together!

Rachel is so excited that all the relatives are coming for latkes on the last night of Hanukkah that she's hopping on one foot as this heartwarming story opens. Soon we meet Mrs. Greenberg, the neighbor with "a heart of gold but [who] is as stubborn as an ox." She won't allow Rachel to borrow potatoes or eggs. Instead, she says, "Borrow? Don't borrow. . . . Eat them in good health." Mrs. Greenberg is alone on Hanukkah, but she refuses Rachel's invitation to come to her house. How Rachel gets Mrs. Greenberg to join in the celebration makes this story one that listeners will thoroughly enjoy while learning about the traditions surrounding this Jewish holiday.

PREREADING FOCUS: Ask: What are some holidays we celebrate in winter? Discuss the traditions surrounding these holidays. When latkes are mentioned, ask how many children have tasted latkes. What do they taste like? What does the word *stubborn* mean? (Unreasonably unyielding; unmoving; want it your way!) Ask for examples of stubborn behavior. Have you ever heard the phrase "stubborn as an ox"? Why do you think an ox might be considered stubborn? Today we are going to read about Rachel and her family as they prepare to celebrate the last night of Hanukkah. Read the title. **Let's read to find out** what the title means.

WHILE READING: Read the first several pages. Ask: What's the most people you've ever had at your house for a celebration? Have you ever been to a party with seventeen people? What would you need? (Lots of space, chairs, big table, and lots of food!) After reading the description of Rachel's home as contrasted to Mrs. Greenberg's home, ask: Which home (Rachel's or Mrs. Greenberg's) would you rather live in? Why? How would you describe your home? Read Mrs. Greenberg's response to Rachel's request for potatoes (and later eggs) with warmth and vigor. After reading the part in which Mrs. Greenberg refuses the invitation, discuss. Ask: Why do you think she chooses not to participate? How do you think she feels as she recalls when she celebrated the last night of Hanukkah as Rachel's mother is doing now? How would you feel if you were Rachel? What can Rachel do? Read on. When Mrs.

Greenberg accepts Rachel's plan, ask: Why does Mrs. Greenberg tell Rachel that she is sweet and smart, with a heart of gold and as stubborn as an ox?

FOLLOW-UP DISCUSSION: Ask: Now that we've read this story, what does the title mean? At the end of the story, why does Rachel say what she does? (That's what Mrs. Greenberg always says to her.) How do you think Mrs. Greenberg feels at the end of the story? How does Rachel feel? Sample latkes! Ask children to draw a picture of a family celebration and write a caption. Or, ask children to draw a picture of their house and describe it as Rachel has described Mrs. Greenberg's and her home in the story.

See Book Notes for additional holiday titles.

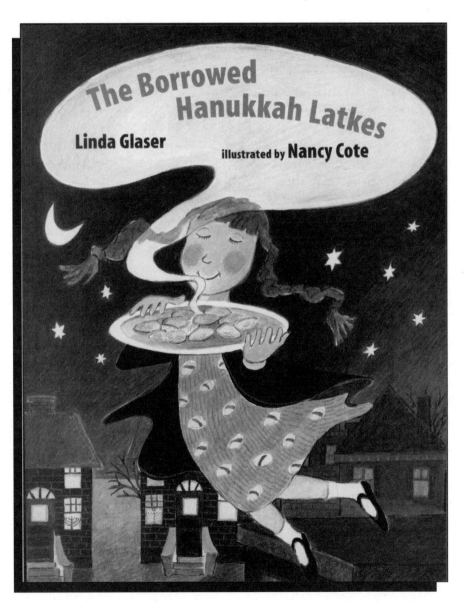

Cover of THE BORROWED HANUKKAH LATKES, copyright 1997, illustrated by Nancy Cote, used with permission of Albert Whitman and Company.

Title	ANIMALS BORN ALIVE AND WELL
Author/Illustrator	Ruth Heller
Publisher	Grosset & Dunlap
Copyright Date	1982
Ages	6–8
Read-Aloud Time	6–8 minutes
Subject . . . . Nonfiction, characteristics and examples of mammals	

Ruth Heller manages to make biology accessible for the youngest of listeners in this lush picture book, one of a series of books that complement one another on the topics of animal and plant life. See below for other titles.

Through rhyming text accompanying accurate, vivid depictions of animals who give birth to live young, we learn that these are MAMMALS, and that they can be found in the sky, in the sea, and all around us on land. As with all the books in this series, the opening and closing pages are the same. In this one we learn that "Winter, spring, summer, fall/a HARE'S hair changes with them all." Clear, straightforward, and simple yet filled with details, this book makes a great addition to a unit on animals.

> **PREREADING FOCUS:** Ask: Who can tell me what a mammal is? (An animal that has fur or hair; they nurse their young; they are born alive with the exception of two—the anteater and the platypus.) Can you name a mammal? **Let's read to find out** more about which animals are mammals and why.

> **WHILE READING:** Take time to explore the illustrations and note the details and the facts presented.

> **FOLLOW-UP DISCUSSION:** Ask children to recall facts from the book about mammals. List them on chart paper. Ask children to illustrate their favorite mammal and write facts about it below their picture. Display. If this read-aloud is part of a unit on animals, be sure to read CHICKENS AREN'T THE ONLY ONES, by Ruth Heller (Putnam). Make webs of different animal kingdom species' characteristics.

Companion titles by Ruth Heller include CHICKENS AREN'T THE ONLY ONES; THE REASON FOR A FLOWER; and PLANTS THAT NEVER EVER BLOOM (Putnam).

For additional nonfiction titles about animals and their characteristics, refer to Book Notes.

Notes:

Title	WHISTLING
Author	Elizabeth Partridge
Illustrator	Anna Grossnickle Hines
Publisher	Greenwillow
Copyright Date	2003
Ages	4–8
Read-Aloud Time	6–8 minutes
Subject	Dad–son bonding, learning to whistle, nature, camping

Note: If you have a hand-sewn quilt you can show children, use it for Follow-up Discussion.

This is a stunning book illustrated with quilts hand sewn by Hines. The story is as quiet as the landscape and as reassuring as a wrap of arms and a warm lap. As Jake works up his resolve with the help of Daddy's encouragement, the sky lightens, the stars disappear, and together they whistle up the sun. Magnificent. Notes on the illustrations at the end of the book explain the process Hines used to make the quilts.

PREREADING FOCUS: Ask: Who can whistle? Was it hard to learn? Discuss students' experiences learning how to whistle. Ask: How would you teach someone to whistle? What advice would you give? Write tips on chart paper. Practice whistling; test tips! Show the cover of the book. Ask: Who are the characters? (A boy and his dad.) What are they doing? (Camping.) Where are they? (In the woods near water in front of a campfire.) What time do you think it is? (Night.) Why? (Dark, stars, campfire.) Ask who has gone camping. Discuss their experiences.

WHILE READING: Read through the first two spreads. Ask: What do you think they are talking about? (Whistling. Clue: title of book.) Read the next two spreads. Dramatize Jake's *whoosh*. What does Jake mean by "too hard" when he tries to whistle? (He let out his breath too hard.) Read the next spread. Ask: Why does Daddy smell that way? (Smoke from campfire; coffee because it's morning; scratchy from the wool of his heavy shirt.) Read the next two spreads. Note the changing sky. Ask: What do we call early morning? (Sunrise; dawn.) Read to the end.

FOLLOW-UP DISCUSSION: Ask: How does Jake feel when he finally whistles? (Joyful!) Review tips the children provided in the Prereading Focus and add tips Daddy gave Jake to the list. Talk about the illustrations and how they were made. Use the notes found at the back of the book to provide facts to share with children. Show children a hand-sewn quilt if you have one available.

See also PIECES: A YEAR IN POEMS & QUILTS, by Anna Grossnickle Hines (Greenwillow).

For another book about camping and bonding at dawn, this time between a boy and his grandfather, see DAWN, by Uri Shulevitz (Farrar, Straus & Giroux).

For more books about family relationships, see Book Notes.

Notes:

Title.	I'M NOT INVITED?
Author/Illustrator	Diana Cain Bluthenthal
Publisher	Atheneum
Copyright Date.	2003
Ages	5–8
Read-Aloud Time	6–8 minutes
Subject . . . . Friends, invitations, being left out, jumping to conclusions	

Note: Have an invitation handy as a prop for this read-aloud.

After school on Tuesday, Minnie overhears a conversation and draws a conclusion. She's not invited to Charles's party. All week long she wonders, worries, and weeps at being left out. From the spelling list of party words, to the annoying bullies in the lunch line, this week would make a party clown frown. In the end, though, Charles emerges from the bushes and clears up Minnie's misconception. It's a fine, fine Saturday after all.

Told with simple, humorous understatement underscored with warm, inviting (ha, ha) watercolors, this story, dedicated to "anyone, or the friend of anyone, who's ever felt left out" is a must-read when the inevitable birthday invitation season begins in your neck of the woods.

PREREADING FOCUS: Hold up an invitation. Ask: What is this? (An invitation.) How do you feel when you get one? How do you feel when you don't get one and others do? Hold up the book. Read the title. Note the question mark at the end. Ask: What do you think this story is about? **Let's read to find out** who this girl is and what she hasn't been invited to.

WHILE READING: Read the first page. What has Minnie heard? (There is a party at 1:00 Saturday at Charles' house.) How does she feel about that? (Happy.) Read through the next two spreads. Use expression as you read Minnie's thoughts. Ask: How is Minnie feeling now? (Sad.) Why? (She hasn't been invited to the party.) Read through the next several spreads. Note details in the illustrations. Ask: How is Minnie feeling as time goes by? (Sadder and sadder.) How do we know Minnie is getting sadder and sadder? (Frowning, making a frown out of her spaghetti, can't concentrate on her spelling words.) Ask: What do you think Minnie ought to do? On Thursday night, Minnie says, "It's okay. I don't have to be invited to everything." What do you think about that? Read the next two spreads. What kind of day is Minnie having? (Frustrating!) Read through the spreads of conversation with Mom. What does Mom mean when she says, "I don't like it when things don't happen either. That's why I'm thankful for tomorrows"? Have you ever felt bad when something didn't happen? Was the next day better? Read on to the end of the story.

FOLLOW-UP DISCUSSION: Ask: How does Minnie feel now? (Happy!) Use this opportunity to discuss invitation etiquette. You may want to send home guidelines for party invitations after discussing them with children. Minnie "jumped to conclusions" about Charles and a party from a piece of conversation she overheard. Ask: What does that mean? What clues did Minnie have that Charles wasn't having a birthday party? (His birthday is in June just like hers.) Do you think it's a good idea to "jump to conclusions"? Have you ever jumped to conclusions? Discuss. What might Minnie have done to solve her problem?

For a follow-up to this book, consider FROM ME TO YOU, written by Anthony France and illustrated by Tiphanie Beeke (Candlewick). See also ANGELINA BALLERINA'S INVITATION TO THE BALLET, written by Katharine Holabird and illustrated by Helen Craig (Pleasant Company).

Title . . . . PARTS
Author/Illustrator . . . . Tedd Arnold
Publisher . . . . Dial
Copyright Date 1997
Ages 4–7
Read-Aloud Time . . . . 6–8 minutes
Subject . . . . Humor, "body parts" we shed, idioms, worrying, taking things literally

It starts with a couple pieces of hair in the comb. Then it's fuzz from the navel—is his stuffing coming out? Is the glue that holds our parts together no longer holding his?? Yikes, this kid's coming unglued. With Arnold's signature bulging eyes the narrator addresses the reader and regales him in rhyme with clues to the ungluing. Be ready for your listeners to be looking for their parts by the end of this hilarious, lighthearted read!

PREREADING FOCUS: Show the cover of the book. Read the title. Ask children what they think this book might be about. Note the character's facial expression, perspiration, and stance. Discuss. Point out the fainter images surrounding the character. Ask: What do you think these have to do with the story? **Let's read to find out**.

WHILE READING: Read the first three spreads. Ask: Is he going bald? (No.) What do you think he's thinking about that little piece of fuzz? Turn the page to find out! Read the next two spreads. Ask: What was that "chunk of something gray and wet" that came from his nose? (Booger!) What do you think he thinks it is? Turn the page to find out! Read the next several spreads without interruption to build toward the resolution at the end.

FOLLOW-UP DISCUSSION: Ask: What other parts could this boy be concerned about? Have children illustrate these! Then read the companions to this book: MORE PARTS and EVEN MORE PARTS: IDIOMS FROM HEAD TO TOE, in which everyday phrases are taken literally by this worrywart. Examples include: "I'll bet that broke your heart," "Please give me a hand," "It's sure to crack you up," . . . you get the idea.

For other books about idioms, look for by Marvin Terban's IN A PICKLE AND OTHER FUNNY IDIOMS (Clarion) and MAD AS A WET HEN! AND OTHER FUNNY IDIOMS (Clarion), both illustrated by Giulio Maestro.

For another humorous look at taking things literally, refer beginning readers to the AMELIA BEDELIA series, written by Peggy Parish and illustrated by Lynn Sweat (HarperCollins).

Notes:

Title	THE PHILHARMONIC GETS DRESSED
Author	Karla Kuskin
Illustrator	Marc Simont
Publisher	HarperCollins
Copyright Date	1982
Ages	4–8
Read-Aloud Time	8–10 minutes
Subject	The philharmonic gets ready for work, instruments, transportation, math

Note: Play a piece of classical music featuring an array of instruments prior to the reading of this book. Consider playing it softly throughout the day! If you have a chart or illustrations of various orchestral instruments, have that handy for follow-up.

It's almost nighttime on a Friday and 105 people are getting ready for work in various ways. Some shower, some bathe in bubbles, some shave, some trim. They all put on their underwear. Detail by detail, we glimpse these musicians readying for their performance and making their way with their instruments to the grand stage. My favorite is the man with "wavy black hair streaked with white like lightning" and a fancy shirt. In the end, the conductor raises his baton and they play. Beautifully. I can almost hear them. Can't you?

> **PREREADING FOCUS:** Play music. Ask: Does anyone know what a "philharmonic" is? (A symphony orchestra.) What instruments do you hear in this piece of music? Show the cover of the book. Ask: What do you do when you get dressed for school? **Let's read to find out** what the philharmonic does when they get dressed for work.

> **WHILE READING:** Read the first two pages. Write "105" on chart paper. Read the next page. If you want to draw the math out of the story, omit the number of women when reading the text and let the students figure it out! (13.) Consider keeping the math figures posted and labeled on chart paper or the board throughout the reading of this book. Read the next two pages. Ask: What size towel do you like to use? Math: If all the men shave except three, how many is that? (89.) If two trim, how many do nothing at all? (One.) Read through the next several pages. Point out *clocks* on the men's hose. Math: If 45 men stand up to put on their trousers, how many do not? (47.) When you get to my favorite member of the philharmonic, ask: What do you think this man does in the orchestra? (Conducts.) Point out a *cummerbund*; ask if anyone has ever seen one. Note that when a man (or woman) wears a tuxedo, he or she usually wears a cummerbund. Math: If eight women wear long skirts, how many do not? (Five.) Ask: Why would bracelets get in the way? Note the illustration. More math: ties, bowties. Keep track of my favorite character! On the spread with the instrument

cases, have children identify what instruments might be in those cases. On the page showing the philharmonic transporting to work, identify the various modes of transportation. Turn to the next page. What is the car waiting for this man called? (Limousine.) Any guesses yet who this man might be? On the spread on which the members of the philharmonic are making their way on stage, identify the instruments. Point out the various large instruments on the next spread. Do the math for the seating. When the children figure out there is one chair or stool short, ask what this means. (One person stands.) Ask who this might be. (Conductor.) What is his job? (Leads the musicians.) Turn the page and read about his job. Read on. On the page on which several of the instruments are listed, point them out in the illustrations.

FOLLOW-UP DISCUSSION: Ask: What new words did we learn today? (These include philharmonic, clocks, suspenders, cummerbund, tails, podium, baton, conductor, symphony, orchestra.) Review the instruments. Ask children if they know anyone who plays an instrument. Ask: What is it, and what does it sound like? Do you have a favorite instrument? What is it, and why is it your favorite? Listen to music and try to identify instruments.

A great follow-up to this book is ZIN! ZIN! ZIN! A VIOLIN, written by Lloyd Moss and illustrated by Marjorie Priceman (Aladdin), in which 10 pieces of the orchestra are described in rhyme and musicians are led by another fanciful conductor, much to the delight of an appreciative audience of expressive animals! A Caldecott Honor book.

Title	AMAZING GRACE
Author	Mary Hoffman
Illustrator	Caroline Binch
Publisher	Dial
Copyright Date	1991
Ages	6–8
Read-Aloud Time	6–8 minutes
Subject	Self-esteem, believing in yourself, drama, family

Grace is amazing. She has an imagination and energy to match her spirit and a family who appreciates her talents. Grace loves stories, and she loves acting them out. She always gives herself the most exciting part, so naturally, when her class plans to perform *Peter Pan*, Grace wants to be Peter. Despite her classmates' negative comments, Grace perseveres with the support of her mother and grandmother. "You can be anything you want, Grace, if you put your mind to it," says Nana, and Grace proves her right. Amazing, indeed, how a little confidence can make you fly. A Reading Rainbow Book.

PREREADING FOCUS: Ask: What does the word *amazing* mean? (Filled with wonder.) What are some amazing things? Discuss. Do you know any people who are amazing? Discuss. Do you ever act out stories you read or hear or see on TV or in a movie or make up in your head? Is it fun? Why? Today we are going to read a story about a girl named Grace who likes to act out stories. Show the cover of the book. The title of the book is AMAZING GRACE. **Let's read to find out** why Grace is amazing.

WHILE READING: As you read the first several pages of the book, note the details of Grace's imaginative play. Note the family members and their participation in Grace's play. When you get to the classroom spread, read the first two lines. Ask: Who do you think Grace wants to be? (Peter Pan.) Read the rest of the spread. Ask: How do you think Grace feels? What do you think Grace will do next? Read the next two pages. Discuss Nana's advice. Ask: What do you think Grace will do? Read the next four pages. Ask: What do you think will happen when Grace auditions? Read on to the end.

FOLLOW-UP DISCUSSION: Ask: Why do you think the author gave the book this title? Discuss Nana's advice and its impact on Grace. Explore student experiences akin to Grace's in which, when they believed in themselves, they met with success.

This book dovetails nicely with STAND TALL, MOLLY LOU MELON, written by Patty Lovell and illustrated by David Catrow (Putnam), another book in which a wise grandmother positively influences her granddaughter's life. See the read-aloud plan found elsewhere in this book.

For a book that can't be beat about a wise grandfather's influence on his grandson's life, read KNOTS ON A COUNTING ROPE, written by Bill Martin Jr. and John Archambault and illustrated by Ted Rand (Holt). See the read-aloud plan found elsewhere in this part of this book.

Notes:

Title	STELLALUNA
Author /Illustrator	Janell Cannon
Publisher	Harcourt
Copyright Date	1993
Ages	6–8
Read-Aloud Time	8–10 minutes
Subject	Friendship despite differences, bat facts

I dare any reader or listener to finish this book and not feel endeared to bats. In that respect it's a lot like CHARLOTTE'S WEB, which will endear you to spiders. With warm illustrations done in acrylics and pencils, Cannon successfully wraps the reader up in the sweetness of her words and the message of her story. Yes, we are different, "But we're friends. And that's a fact." Stellaluna's got it right. "Bat Notes" follow the story for those interested in additional facts about these intriguing mammals.

PREREADING FOCUS: Show the cover of the book. Ask children what animal this is. (Bat.) What is unusual about this illustration? (Bats hang upside down; they don't perch.) Point out birds in the background. Ask for predictions on what this story might be about. Read the title. Ask: What do you think the title means? (It is the bat's name.) **Let's read to find out** what facts we learn about bats from the story.

WHILE READING: Read the first page. Discuss why Mother Bat may have named her baby Stellaluna. (Luna means moon, and bats fly at night.) If no one comes up with this answer, leave the question and return to it at the end of the story. Read the first three spreads. Ask: How do you think Stellaluna is feeling? Where do you think her mother is? What facts have we learned about bats so far? List these on chart paper. (Bats search for food at night. Fruit bats eat fruit. The owl is enemy to the bat. Bats hang upside down by their feet.) Read the next three spreads. Ask: Why didn't Stellaluna like the bugs? (Fruit bats eat fruit.) What did Stellaluna learn to do from the birds? (She stayed awake in the day and slept at night. She ate bugs.) What did Stellaluna teach the birds? (To hang by their feet.) Why do you think this upset Mama when she returned to the nest? (It's dangerous for birds to hang by their feet.) Read the next six spreads. Ask: What do you think will happen next? Read on through Stellaluna's reunion with Mama and the eating of the fruit. Review the bat ways Stellaluna relearned. Read the last three spreads to the end of the story.

FOLLOW-UP DISCUSSION: Ask: What do you think is the most important thing Stellaluna learned? (Friends can be different and feel different but still be friends.) Illustrate bat facts and post them around the room. Explain Stellaluna's name. (See above.) Use "Bat Notes" at the back of the book at your discretion.

For the flip side opinion on an affection for bug confection, see the award-winning nonfiction book, BUGS FOR LUNCH, written by Margery Facklam and illustrated by Sylvia Long (Charlesbridge). Through simple rhyme accompanied by illustrations done in pen and ink and watercolors, we learn about creatures that enjoy munching bugs for lunch—including a bat.

For nonfiction books about animals, refer to Book Notes.

Notes:

Title . . . . COCK-A-DOODLE DUDLEY	
Author /Illustrator . . . . Bill Peet	
Publisher . . . . Houghton Mifflin	
Copyright Date 1990	
Ages 6–9	
Read-Aloud Time . . . . 10–15 minutes	
Subject . . . . Spirit, enthusiasm, friendship, jealousy, bullies	

Note: Prepare sheets for follow-up writing activity.

The barnyard is in an uproar when the jealous brute of a goose Gunther deems Dudley, the fabulous crower, a fake. "Oh no! Not Dudley! No, no!" cry the barnyard friends. But honest Dudley comes clean, admitting that his crowing is not magic; it does not make the sun rise. "I'm just a plain, ordinary rooster," he claims. But about this he's wrong. Sol the sun and his barnyard buddies show him—and readers—just how special Dudley is. With spunky language and expressive, comical illustrations, this story is sure to delight reader and listeners alike.

PREREADING FOCUS: Show the cover of the book. Read the title. Ask: Who do you think Cock-A-Doodle Dudley is? (Rooster.) Open the book to reveal the span of front and back covers. Ask: What do roosters do? (Crow at sunrise.) **Let's read to find out** more about this character.

WHILE READING: Read through page 9. Ask: Why do you think Dudley is Sol's favorite rooster? (Spirited and enthusiastic.) Read through page 13. Ask: Why doesn't Gunther like Dudley? (He's jealous.) What does that mean? Discuss. Read through page 21. How do the barnyard fellows feel toward Gunther? (Scornful.) Why? (He's grumpy and jealous.) What do you think Dudley will say? Read through page 25. Why do you think that Dudley is as popular as ever? (He's likable.) Read through page 35. Ask: What do you think will happen in the morning if Sol doesn't come up? What do you think will happen to Dudley in the dark, spooky woods? Read on through page 45. Ask: Who were Dudley's enemies in the woods? (Fox and owl.) Why? (They wanted to eat him.) Why didn't Dudley answer Hector? (He was hiding from the owl.) What do you think will happen next? Read to the end.

FOLLOW-UP DISCUSSION: Ask: Why do you think Dudley was so popular in the barnyard? (He was friendly and likable.) Who was your favorite barnyard buddy in the story? Why? Hand out prepared sheets on which children will write out why they like Dudley, as if they are one of the barnyard characters. Ask children to illustrate their papers. Sheets read: Dudley is my friend because . . . . Signed, _____ .

See the read-aloud plan for STAND TALL, MOLLY LOU MELON, written by Patty Lovell and illustrated by David Catrow (Putnam), found elsewhere in this part of this book, for a good companion to this story.

See Book Notes and Tips and Techniques for Teachers and Librarians for additional books on the subject of bullies and friendship.

COCK-A-DOODLE DUDLEY. Reprinted by permission of Houghton Mifflin.

Notes:

Title	HOME AT LAST
Author	Susan Middleton Elya
Illustrator	Felipe Davalos
Publisher	Lee & Low
Copyright Date	2002
Ages	6–8
Read-Aloud Time	6–8 minutes
Subject	Learning a new language, adjusting to a new culture, family, home

Eight-year old Ana and her family have moved to the United States from Mexico. Although the transition to her new surroundings is exciting for Ana, she senses it is not as easy for her mother, who misses home. Spanish words and phrases are interspersed throughout this story of Ana's mother's gradual assimilation into her new country. With Ana's help Mama eventually finds her way home. Rich oil illustrations complement the warmth of this story of family and home.

PREREADING FOCUS: Show the cover of the book. Read the title. Ask: What do you think the title means? What does it take for a place to be called "home"? Discuss. Have you ever traveled to a new place? Did you ever visit a place that seemed strange or different, or a place where you didn't know anyone? How did you feel? Discuss. Do you think it would be hard to go to another country to live? Why? What would make it hard? Discuss. **Let's read to find out** about Ana and her family's experiences with their new home in America.

WHILE READING: Read the first page. Ask: What have we learned about Ana and her family so far? (They have moved to the United States from Mexico. Ana is eight years old; her mother misses Mexico; they live in a rural area in an apartment on the third floor. Ana has twin baby brothers named Jesus and Julio. Ana's father and uncle work in a canning factory.) What is a canning factory? (A place where food is placed in cans to be sold in stores.) How does Ana know her mother misses Mexico? (She looks out the window and sighs.) Read the next three pages. Ask: How are things going at school for Ana? (She likes it.) How are things going for her father? (Well.) When Ana suggests to her mother that she learn English, Mama says, "Imposible!" Why? (She doesn't think she can learn English.) Do you think she can? Read the next two pages. Ask: How are things different here? (Odd packages, strange words, no one speaks Spanish.) Read the next several pages. Ask: Why does Mama decide to learn to speak English? (She realizes it is important after Jesus gets ill.) Read to the end of the book.

FOLLOW-UP DISCUSSION: At the end of the book, Mama says, "We're home." Ask: Why does Mama feel at home now? (She has learned to speak English and was able to stand up for herself to the grocer who had not understood her and overcharged her for chicken earlier in the story.) How does Ana feel? (Happy.) How did Ana help her mother? (She supported and encouraged her mother.) If someone new moved into your neighborhood or came to your school, what could you do to help that person feel welcome?

For a story about a child's first day of school in a new country, read SUMI'S FIRST DAY OF SCHOOL EVER, written by Soyung Pak and illustrated by Joung Un Kim (Viking). For an enchanting tale about a Chinese boy's new life on the California coast where he works with his uncle as a fisherman, read ORANGES ON GOLD MOUNTAIN, written by Elizabeth Partridge and illustrated by Aki Sogabe (Penguin).

HOME AT LAST. Reprinted with permission from Lee & Low Books (leeandlow.com).

Notes:

Title . . . . ALBERT
Author. . . . . Donna Jo Napoli
Illustrator . . . . Jim LaMarche
Publisher. . . . . Harcourt
Copyright Date 2001
Ages . . . . 6 and up
Read-Aloud Time . . . . 6–8 minutes
Subject . . . . Overcoming fear, living life

Note: For follow-up activity, have a bird's nest and small strips of paper ready.

Donna Jo Napoli is the award-winning author of many books for older children. This is her first picture book. In this tale on many levels, Albert learns through chance and a nest built in his hand by two cardinals that life is both good and bad, and it is worth living and enjoying. And he learns to like the taste of beetles, too. Inviting illustrations in colored pencil on watercolor paper capture the spirit and meaning of Napoli's words.

PREREADING FOCUS: Show the cover of the book. Read the title. Ask: Who do you think Albert is? What details do you notice here? (Cardinal, twig, city in background, Albert's pensive expression.) **Let's read to find out** why this cardinal is on this man's head.

WHILE READING: Read the first page. Ask: What noises did Albert hear? (People in apartment above, dog next door, children giggling, garbage truck rumbling by.) What was the weather like? (Too cold.) Read the next two pages. Ask the same questions. Also: Does Albert ever go out? (No.) Why not? (Weather; doesn't like noises.) Read the next several pages in which Albert stands at the window. Ask: Would Albert have considered the man and woman yelling a good noise or a bad noise? (Bad.) Why did he smile later? (The man and woman made up and laughed and hugged and gave each other a present.) Read the next page. How has Albert helped the birds? (Holding the nest, breathing warm air on the eggs, shooing away the cat.) Read the next several pages. How does Albert help the last bird? What advice does he give him? ("Go for it . . . . Give it a try.") When the last bird flies away, Albert has learned something. What has he learned? (That both the good and the bad noises are part of this world, of life.) How is the weather in Albert's opinion now? (Just right.) Read the last page.

FOLLOW-UP DISCUSSION: At the end of the book, we read that sometimes Albert flies. How does he do this? (On a swing.) Which cardinal might this be on his head? (The last one he helped learn to fly.) What did Albert learn from helping the cardinals? (Life lessons.) Do you think Albert is happier now? (Yes.) Why? Fill a nest with slips of paper, on which children have written things they are afraid of—the "bad noises" of life. Like Albert and the last baby cardinal, they can let their cares "fly away"!

Notes:

Title	THE MOTHER'S DAY MICE
Author	Eve Bunting
Illustrator	Jan Brett
Publisher	Clarion
Copyright Date	1986
Ages	6 and up
Read-Aloud Time	6–8 minutes
Subject	Mother's Day

Note: Copy Little Mouse's song onto chart paper for the follow-up activity. Keep it out of sight prior to the read-aloud!

Biggest Little Mouse wakes first. It's Mother's Day, and it's time to go for presents. With Middle Mouse and Little Mouse he sets out across the meadow "long as a snake," past a red fox and an owl, into the strawberry patch. While Middle Mouse picks the roundest, reddest berry, Biggest Mouse selects a dandelion fluff ball, a "wish flower for Mother." Little Mouse hopes for honeysuckle for Mother, but Cat is on the porch of Honeysuckle Cottage listening to someone playing the piano inside. While they hide, hoping Cat will leave, the "beat" of an idea forms in Little Mouse's mind for the perfect gift he will bring to his mother. A sweet, simple story accompanied by bright illustrations brimming with details.

PREREADING FOCUS: Ask: What gift could you give your mother on Mother's Day? What gift might a mouse give its mother on Mother's Day? **Let's read to find out** what gifts Biggest, Middle, and Little Mouse give to their mother this Mother's Day.

WHILE READING: Read the first page. Ask: What day is it? (Mother's Day.) Where do you think they will head for gifts? Read the next page. Ask: What time of day is it? (Night, just before dawn.) Who do you think lives in Honeysuckle Cottage? Read the next spread. Find the snake in the grass. Ask: Why didn't Little Mouse want to think about snakes? (They are enemies to mice.) Read the next spread. Find the fox and owl. Ask: Is Little Mouse frightened? (Yes.) How do you know? (His voice is weak; he keeps his eyes closed tight; he squeezes Middle Mouse's tail hard.) Read the next two spreads. Ask: What does Middle Mouse pick for Mother? (Round, red strawberry.) Why does Mother love strawberries? (The first ones taste of summer coming.) What does Biggest Mouse pick for Mother? (A dandelion fluff ball.) Read the next several spreads. Find the moth and the beetle. Ask: What do you think Little Mouse's idea for a gift might be? Read through to the end of the story. Find the frog. Ask: What do you think Mother wished for when she blew on the fluff ball? Have you ever made a wish on a dandelion fluff ball? Why does Mother say the song is better than honeysuckle? (It lasts forever.)

FOLLOW-UP DISCUSSION: At the end of the story, what is the kitchen filled with? (Warm wishes, summer coming, music, and love.) Why those things? (From the fluff ball, the strawberry, the song, their gifts to their mother.) Sing Little Mouse's song together to the tune of "Twinkle, Twinkle, Little Star," using the verse printed on the chart paper!

For additional holiday titles, refer to Book Notes.

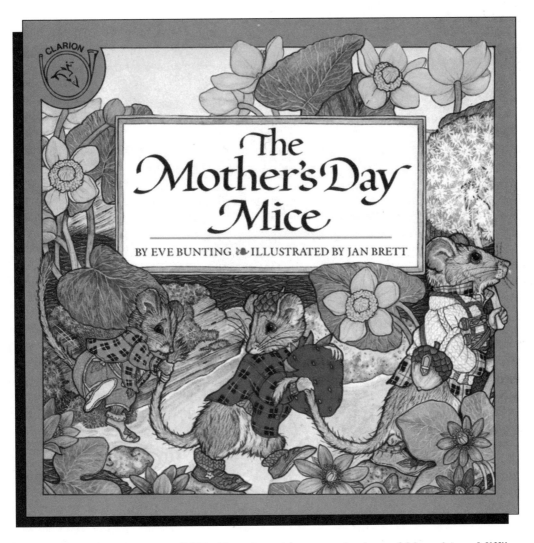

THE MOTHER'S DAY MICE. Reprinted by permission of Houghton Mifflin.

Notes:

Title	DON'T FORGET THE BACON!
Author/Illustrator	Pat Hutchins
Publisher	Greenwillow
Copyright Date	1976
Ages	6 and up
Read-Aloud Time	5–7 minutes
Subject	Word play

Note: Prepare the boy's list on chart paper as written on the first page of the story.

In this book, Pat Hutchins, the author/artist famous for meaty stories that feature comic illustrations and very few words, offers a trip to the market that listeners will not soon forget. The story opens with a mother telling her son what she needs from the market. Look at the expression on his face and you'll know what the problem will be here. Six farm eggs become six fat legs. A cake for tea becomes a cape for me. A pound of pears becomes a flight of stairs. Will he forget the bacon?

PREREADING FOCUS: Ask: Have you ever been given a list of things to buy or do for your mom or dad? Was it written? Were you ever given a list of things to buy or do that you just were expected to remember without a written list? Is that hard to do? Discuss. Today we're going to read about a boy who is given a list of things to buy for his mom. It's not a written list, though, so **Let's read to find out** what happens!

WHILE READING: Be sure to read the pages prior to the first page of the story. Ask: What do you think is the most important thing he has to buy? (Bacon.) Why? (Title of story; she repeats it.) Read the first page. Go over the list on chart paper. As you continue to read, have the children correct the boy's mistakes by reading from the chart paper what he is supposed to buy for his mother. Midway through the story, ask: Do you think he'll forget the bacon? Pay attention to the details in the illustrations, such as the dog and butterfly, the merchant's face, and how the boy remembers what he is supposed to bring home!

FOLLOW-UP DISCUSSION: Ask: What happens at the end of the story? (He is heading back for the bacon!) Do you think he will remember? Make up a new shopping list. Ask children to come up with silly things you might bring home instead!

For other examples of magnificent word play, read SILLY SALLY, by Audrey Wood (Harcourt); CLOUDY WITH A CHANCE OF MEATBALLS, written by Judi Barrett and illustrated by Ron Barrett (Atheneum); and LOCUST POCUS! A BOOK TO BUG YOU, written by Douglas Kaine McKelvey and illustrated by Richard Egielski (Philomel).

Notes:

Title	THE ANT AND THE ELEPHANT
Author/Illustrator	Bill Peet
Publisher	Houghton Mifflin
Copyright Date	1972
Ages	5 and up
Read-Aloud Time	10–15 minutes
Subject	Attitude; good deeds; manners

Through expressive illustrations and zippy text, we meet a medley of irascible, ungrateful slugs of the wilderness that don't know how to be a friend or thank a stranger for acts of kindness. Playful word wit and humorous depictions of animals with human qualities are Peet's signature, as is a pointed message that somehow never hits you between the eyes with its moral. In this story we have a "snooty" giraffe "gallopity-clopping away" and an elephant and 95,000 ants "herumpity-bumpity clumpity-hump . . . off through the jungle together." I repeat: Peet can't be beat. Good thing he was so prolific.

> **PREREADING FOCUS:** Ask: Which two animals of the jungle would you say are the most opposite? Why? Show the cover of the book but hide the title. Ask: What animals do you see on the cover of this book? Show the title and read it. **Let's read to find out** how these two got together.

> **WHILE READING:** Note the nicknames Peet gives to the various animals we encounter. Discuss. Note the lack of concern for others in the first half of the story and the lack of gratitude toward the elephant in the latter half of the story. Discuss the elephant's reaction to the rudeness of the various animals. When you get to the page from which the cover is taken, be sure to point it out. When the elephant meets with trouble, what is he doing that causes him not to pay attention? (Being prideful about his many good deeds; think: *Pride goeth before a fall!*)

> **FOLLOW-UP DISCUSSION:** Ask: What lesson has the elephant learned in this story? (Not to be pleased with himself for all his good deeds.) Why do you think the ant helped the elephant? (The elephant rescued him earlier.) Do you think the ant might have helped the elephant even if the elephant hadn't helped him? Discuss. Why did the ant bring along 95,000 friends? (The elephant's a big fellow!) What do you think would have happened if the giraffe, the rhino, or the lion had come along before the ant? Reread the last line of the story. Who is the "mighty big" and who is the "mighty small"? (Elephant; ants.)

For additional titles on manners, see Book Notes.

For another great title by Peet, see the read-aloud plan for COCK-A-DOODLE DUDLEY found elsewhere in this part of this book.

THE ANT AND THE ELEPHANT. Reprinted by permission of Houghton Mifflin.

Notes:

Title . . . . KNOTS ON A COUNTING ROPE
Author . . . . Bill Martin Jr. and John Archambault
Illustrator . . . . Ted Rand
Publisher . . . . Holt
Copyright Date 1987
Ages . . . . 6 and up
Read-Aloud Time . . . . 8–10 minutes
Subject . . . . Grandfatherly love and wisdom, blindness, Navajo culture

Note: Have a one- to two-foot length of thin rope with a knot in it on hand for the telling of this story. Cut one-foot lengths of rope for each child to take home following the reading of this story. See the follow-up activity.

"Tell me the story again, Grandfather/Tell me who I am." So begins this tale, and as we hear it, as the boy hears it again, another knot is formed on the counting rope. Step by step we learn of the boy's tenuous birth and then the childhood of Boy-Strength-of-Blue-Horses, the name given him by his gruff but loving grandfather. Through verse that sparks the senses, we hear the conversation between the two, the recounting of the boy's life, first by Grandfather, then by grandson. Eventually we learn of the boy's blindness and then witness his growing confidence at the hand of his grandfather, his teacher, his support, by way of splendid spreads. At the end we learn the meaning of the title and the strength to be found in abiding love. A treasure of a book, a book to treasure.

PREREADING FOCUS: Show the cover of the book. Read the title. Ask: What can you tell me about this story from looking at the cover and reading the title? (Native American story, rope with knots, grandfather and grandson.) Tell children that these characters are Navajo. Show on a map where Navajos live. Ask: What do you think these characters are doing? What do you think a counting rope might be? **Let's read to find out**.

WHILE READING: Look at the title page. Ask: Where do you think this story takes place? (Desert climate.) How do you know? (Terrain.) Read the first page. Use expression and change tone or cadence to convey the conversation taking place between the two. Ask: What story does the boy want his grandfather to tell? (About who he is, his life) Read the next page. Ask: What do you think a *hogan* is? (Navajo Indian dwelling made of logs and mud; door faces east.) What kind of night was it? (Windy.) Read the next page. Ask: What custom do the Navajos have when a baby is born? (A grandmother must bless him.) How is the wind described? (Wounded; whipping up sand as sharp as claws; crying like a bobcat.) List these on chart paper. What does "heart-pounding afraid" mean? Read the next three pages of text. Ask: Do you know how you got your name? Discuss. Read the next two pages. Ask: What have we learned about Boy-Strength-of-Blue-Horses? (He is blind.) When his grandfather describes blue, the boy says he can see it. Why? (It is the things he feels and loves.) Read the next page. Ask: Why did the boy name his foal Rainbow? (A rainbow appeared when it was born.) How do you think he knew that? How do you think Circles got her name? Read the next page. Ask: How did the boy train his horse? (With the help of his grandfather.) Read about the race. Ask: The boy says the wind is his friend. Why? (It throws back his hair and laughs in his face.) Add these to the list on chart paper. Why wasn't the boy afraid at the end of the race? (He could see through the dark.) His grandfather says, "You were crossing dark mountains, Boy!" What does he mean? (He has overcome his fear and his handicap.) Grandfather says the boy didn't win the race but he won anyway. What does he mean? (He has overcome darkness.) Read the last page of the story. Ask: What does the title means?

FOLLOW-UP DISCUSSION: Boy-Strength-of-Blue-Horses got his name from his grandfather because of something that happened soon after his birth. Then he grew into his name. Horses were important. He grew strong. Ask: If you were Navajo, what name do you think you would have? Why? Draw pictures of Navajo-inspired names. Ask children to ask their parent(s) how they got their names and be ready to tell their classmates tomorrow. Give each child a rope. The first knot will be the story they hear tonight.

For two more titles that explore the experience of being blind, read THROUGH GRANDPA'S EYES, written by Patricia MacLachlan and illustrated by Deborah Kogan Ray (HarperCollins), and NAOMI KNOWS IT'S SPRINGTIME, written by Virginia L. Kroll and illustrated by Jill Kastner (Boyds Mills Press).

For an account of a guide dog's day, read the story based on fact, LOOKING OUT FOR SARAH, by Glenna Lang (Charlesbridge).

For additional titles about family relationships, see Book Notes.

Cover of KNOTS ON A COUNTING ROPE, copyright 1987 by Ted Rand, used with permission of Henry Holt and Company.

Title . . . . HERE'S WHAT YOU CAN DO WHEN YOU CAN'T FIND YOUR SHOE	
Author . . . . Andrea Perry	
Illustrator . . . . Alan Snow	
Publisher . . . . Atheneum	
Copyright Date 2003	
Ages . . . . 7 and up	
Read-Aloud Time . . . . 10–15 minutes	
Subject . . . . Silly inventions, poetry, humor	

Note: You may want to precede the reading of this book with a read-aloud of SO YOU WANT TO BE AN INVENTOR?, written by Judith St. George and illustrated by David Small (Philomel), either on a previous day or earlier in the day on which you read this book aloud. Short, spiffy profiles of some of the best and the brightest, including well-known (Ben Franklin and Thomas Alva Edison) and lesser-known (Josephine Cochran, inventor of the first dishwasher, and Joseph Henry, the man who invented a telegraph system fourteen years before Samuel F. B. Morse!) inventors. Brief and funny biographical sketches are accompanied by the spunky illustrations of David Small, who won the Caldecott Medal for the similarly formatted SO YOU WANT TO BE PRESIDENT?, also written by St. George.

Another option is to spread the reading of these poems over several days leading up to the launch of a science/invention unit.

There isn't a better book to introduce an invention convention or science fair in your classroom or school than this one. Subtitled "Ingenious Inventions for Pesky Problems," this collection of poems explains the "sure-footed shoe finder," the "tooth-fairy forklift," what a "stink stopper" is, and how a "spider spotter" works. By the time you finish reading these hilarious poems, your budding inventors will be ready to launch the lunchroom monitor or improve the food in the cafeteria. Who knows??

PREREADING FOCUS: Ask: What is an invention? Why are inventions important? What inventions couldn't you do without? Are there inventions you think we need? Discuss.

WHILE READING: Read the title of each poem and study the illustration before reading the verse aloud. Discuss what the invention might be and what pesky problem it might solve.

FOLLOW-UP DISCUSSION: Ask children to name their favorite invention in the book and tell why. Discuss which invention would probably work best. Which one has serious faults? Which is funniest? Weirdest? Grossest? Which one would appeal to the most people? To the fewest number of people? Who might use each invention? Of the inventors we've read about, who might have invented each of these inventions? Ready, set, go! Set your scientists loose!

For additional poetry books, refer to Tips and Techniques for Teachers and Librarians.

Notes:

| Title | . . . . | THE STORY OF FROG BELLY RAT BONE |

Title . . . . THE STORY OF FROG BELLY RAT BONE
Author/Illustrator . . . . Timothy Basil Ering
Publisher . . . . Candlewick
Copyright Date 2003
Ages . . . . 7 and up
Read-Aloud Time . . . . 8–10 minutes
Subject . . . . The environment, plants versus cement

Note: Have bright packets of seeds and an assortment of cans, jars, and boxes filled with soil ready for your crew to plant after reading this tale. (Not that your classroom looks anything like Cementland!) If you have a small treasure chest, place seeds inside. Keep it closed until you have finished reading the story.

Frog Belly Rat Bone is made from trash. His purpose in life is to guard a boy's treasure—tiny gray specks sprinkled from bright packets into holes, jars, cans, and boxes all over dull, dreary Cementland. With patience and pluck, Frog Belly Rat Bone and the boy gradually transform the trampled, dingy landscape into a bright, sprite wonderland of flowers and veggies galore. Enough for a feast fit for a king and his friends. Three cheers for Frog Belly Rat Bone. Three cheers for this tale illustrated in acrylic and hand-lettered by the author/illustrator. A perfect pick for Earth Day.

PREREADING FOCUS: Ask: What happens to the trash you put at the curb on garbage day? (Trucks come and take it away.) Discuss garbage, trash, and recycling. Ask: What is a dump? (Where trash is collected.) Have you ever seen one? What would you find in a dump? What do you think a dump smells like? Show the cover of the book and read the title. Ask: Which character on the cover do you think is Frog Belly Rat Bone? Why? **Let's read to find out** more about a dump.

WHILE READING: Show the inside cover of the book. Discuss its color and feel. Note the lone flower. Look at the next page. What's different? (Color, fruit, firefly.) Read the first page. Ask: What kind of treasure would you like to find? Read the next two pages. Ask: What do you think he spied? Read the next two spreads. Ask: What were all the wondrous riches? (Seeds.) Read the next page. Ask: Why hasn't anything happened? (It takes time for seeds to sprout.) Read the next three pages. Ask: What is he making? (A scarecrow. Frog Belly Rat Bone!) Why? (To scare away the thieves.) Read the next several spreads through the scene of the fleeing thieves and the sprouting of the first of the wondrous riches. Note changing color. Read the next spread. Ask: What do you think will happen next? Read and revel in the final spreads of the story.

FOLLOW-UP DISCUSSION: Ask: How does Cementland look now? Compare end papers from the front and back and the first and last few spreads. Present the treasure box. Ask: What do you think is in here? (Wondrous riches!) Open the box, open the packets, plant the seeds, and be patient!

This book would make a great duo paired with a Johnny Appleseed title. See JOHNNY APPLESEED, retold and illustrated by Steven Kellogg (HarperCollins).

Or, for a different approach, follow the reading of this tale with FREDERICK, by Leo Lionni (Random House), in which one mouse's words are the wondrous riches that lighten and brighten dreary winter for his field mice friends.

For additional tales, fairy tales, fractured fairy tales, folk tales, and legends, see Book Notes.

THE STORY OF FROG BELLY RATE BONE © 2003 by Timothy Basil Ering. Reproduced by permission of the publisher Candlewick Press, Inc., Cambridge, MA.

Notes:

Title	MATH-TERPIECES
Author	Greg Tang
Illustrator	Greg Paprocki
Publisher	Scholastic
Copyright Date	2003
Ages	5 and up
Read-Aloud Time	3–35 minutes*
Subject	Math problem-solving, addition, art masterpieces, art history, poetry

Time involved depends on whether you read the entire book in one sitting or solve problems singly.

Note: To prepare for suggested follow-up activity, assemble a collection of illustrations of art masterpieces.

In the fifth book in his series, Tang says in his author's note that his goal is to "create math problems that teach, challenge, inspire, and entertain," and he has accomplished all that in style. With a bright, appealing, interactive collection of art masterpieces accompanied by poems, Tang poses math problems involving addition, probability, permutations, and thinking strategies. Solutions, strategies for solving problems, and art notes are found at the end of the book. That's a lot to pack into a book for the five- to ten-year-old, but Tang does it with aplomb. Math jettisons from dullsville to dynamic between the covers of this sunny yellow book.

> **PREREADING FOCUS:** Show the cover of the book. Read the title. Ask: What do you think this book is about? (Math and art masterpieces.) **Let's read to find out** how the author connects the two.

> **WHILE READING:** Read each selection and do the math. Identify the artist and title of each masterpiece. Discuss its qualities. For more on the art style, consult notes found at the end of the book.

> **FOLLOW-UP DISCUSSION:** Ask children to select an art masterpiece and make up a problem in the style of the book. Share and solve results. Display around the room or math center.

Consider pairing the problem using Warhol's famous Campbell's Soup Can: Tomato 1968 (pp. 26–27) with UNCLE ANDY'S, by James Warhola (Putnam). See the read-aloud plan found elsewhere in this part of this book.

See also MATH FOR ALL SEASONS, the second book in this series by Tang (illustrated by Harry Briggs) for riddles that encourage creative problem solving by grouping and adding, subtracting to add, and looking for patterns. Appropriate for five- to eight-year-olds.

For a listing of other math-related books, see Book Notes and Tips and Techniques for Teachers and Librarians.

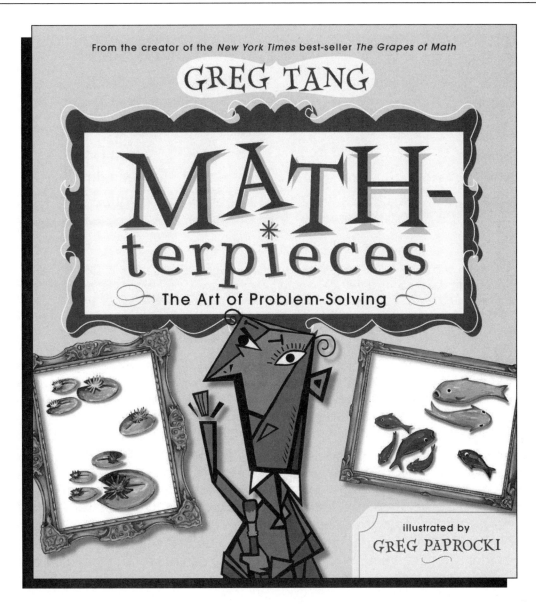

Illustration by Greg Paprocki from MATH-TERPIECES by Greg Tang. Illustration copyright © 2003 by Gregory Tang. Used by permission of Scholastic Inc.

Notes:

Title . . . . THE DOORBELL RANG
Author/Illustrator . . . . Pat Hutchins
Publisher . . . . Greenwillow
Copyright Date 1986
Ages . . . . 5 and up
Read-Aloud Time . . . . 5–7 minutes
Subject . . . . Sharing, simple division, friends and neighbors

Note: For a fun and filling follow-up activity, arrange enough chocolate chip cookies for each child to have two, or three, or six on a tray like Grandma's! (You may want to get the mini-sized cookies.) Count, divide, and enjoy! For even more fun, plan for a group of children from another classroom to knock on the door just as your children are about to eat their cookies. Arrange for the number of children at the door to divide evenly into the number of cookies on hand! Count, divide, and enjoy!

Pat Hutchins is a master at economy of words. Consider her picture book, ROSIE'S WALK, which has managed to remain in print for decades. It's a mere 32 words. And here she successfully and painlessly introduces everyday math involving simple division in a story about sharing Ma's scrumptious chocolate chip cookies. They look and smell as good as Grandma's, insist the kids, even though Ma repeats throughout the tale, "No one makes cookies like Grandma." They look and smell so good, though, that as the doorbell rings on the right-hand page of each spread, it's hard to miss the growing dismay on the children's faces as their share of the chippy wonders dwindles. There's twelve divided by two, then four, then six, then twelve. When the doorbell rings the final time, the tension mounts over successive spreads. What to do? Don't answer? Eat quickly? But all is well. It's Grandma on the other side of the door with a bountiful tray of cookies. Plenty for everyone. Hooray, hooray. Who can resist counting the cookies and figuring out how many each child gets now?

> **PREREADING FOCUS:** Show the cover of the book and read the title. Ask: What would you do if you were about to have a snack and the doorbell rang? What would you do if there weren't enough for everyone? Count the number of children on the cover of the book. (12.) What do we call twelve of one thing? (A dozen.) **Let's read to find out** what happens when the doorbell rings at this house.

> **WHILE READING:** Read the first page. Ask: How many cookies are there on the plate? (12.) When there is 12 of something, what do we call it? (A dozen.) If these two are going to share the cookies, how many could each one have? (Six.) Read the next two pages. Ask: What do you think will happen now? Read the next spread. Ask: Now how many cookies will each child have? (Three.) Read the next spread. Ask children what Ma says when the children say they smell as good as Grandma's. ("No one makes cookies like Grandma.") Read the next spread. Ask: Now how many cookies will each child have? (Two.) How are the children feeling about that? Read the next spread. Ask the children to

read what Ma says when the children say the cookies look as good as Grandma's. ("No one makes cookies like Grandma.") Read the next spread. Ask: How many children are at the door? (Six.) How many children are there in all? (12.) How many cookies each is that? (One.) What do you think will happen next? Read the next two spreads. Ask: What do you think the children should do? Read the next spread. Ask: How will they share the cookies now? Turn the page and see who it is! Read to the end. On the last page, ask the children what Ma says before reading it aloud. ("No one makes cookies like Grandma.") As you read this aloud, point to each word.

FOLLOW-UP DISCUSSION: Count the number of cookies on Grandma's tray and divide by the number of children. How many cookies will each child have now? (Tricky! Don't forget the one they already have from Ma's batch! I count 60 on the tray. Six cookies each.) If there are enough for six cookies each, what part of a *dozen* is that? (One-half.) Note that this is the number of cookies each child was to have at the start of the story! Bring out a tray of cookies. Count and divide! See note above.

For another book about the concept of a dozen, read ONE CARTON OF OOPS!, written by Judy Bradbury and illustrated by Cathy Trachok (McGraw-Hill), in which Christopher goes to the store to buy a carton of eggs for his mother and a series of mishaps ensues on the way home.

For additional math-related books, see Book Notes and Tips and Techniques for Teachers and Librarians.

Notes:

Title . . . . UNCLE ANDY'S	
Author/Illustrator . . . . James Warhola	
Publisher . . . . Putnam	
Copyright Date 2003	
Ages . . . . 6 and up	
Read-Aloud Time . . . . 7–10 minutes	
Subject . . . . Andy Warhol, art	

Note: Find examples of pop art, especially Warhol's soup can paintings, to share with the children. A picture of one of Warhol's soup cans be found in MATH-TERPIECES, written by Greg Tang and illustrated by Greg Paprocki (Scholastic), for which a read-aloud plan can be found elsewhere in this part of this book.

Subtitled "A faabbbulous visit with Andy Warhol," this book by Warhol's nephew introduces the young listener to the pop artist and his incredible art, which focuses on everyday things. The author shares an inside look at this American icon's life and home from the viewpoint of a devoted nephew who learned about art on his memorable visits to his uncle's house in New York City. In the author's note, Warhola refers to these visits as "great adventure[s] to a very exotic land." This story focuses on a visit that took place in 1962, the year Warhol unveiled his soup can paintings.

> **PREREADING FOCUS:** Show children a picture one of Andy Warhol's soup can paintings. Ask: Have you ever seen this painting? Did you know this is a famous painting by an American artist? His name is Andy Warhol, and this is called *pop art*, which means art that shows everyday, ordinary things. Show other examples of pop art to the children. Today we are going to read a story about a visit to Andy Warhol's house in New York City written by his nephew. Show the cover and point to the author/illustrator's name. There is only one name on the cover of this book. Do you know what this means? (Warhola also illustrated the book.) The visit to Uncle Andy's took place in 1962 when the author was a young boy. **Let's read to find out** more about the author/illustrator's visit with his famous uncle, Andy Warhol.

> **WHILE READING:** Read the first page. Ask: Do you think it would be fun to have a yard like this? Why? What is a junkyard? What would you find there? Discuss the ups and downs of having a yard that looks like a junkyard. Read the next several pages about the author's dad. Ask: What would your mother say if your yard looked like this? Would you like to have a dad who makes art by putting a bunch of things together in interesting ways? What would you make? What would you use to make it? Would you like playing in the junk in James's yard? Read about the preparation for the trip. Ask: Have you ever gone on a car trip? What do you do to get ready for a car trip? Note how many children are in the car! Read the next page. Contrast the city with the author's home. How do you think James felt when they drove into New York City? Read the next page. Discuss James's bed and the idea of a surprise visit of eight guests! Read the next

page. Ask: How did James know that the soup boxes were really important? (Uncle Andy told them not to touch any of it.) Read and study the illustrations on the next several pages. Note unique characteristics of Uncle Andy and his home. (25 cats named Sam; his reaction to junk; the layout of the house and it contents.) Ask: Why do you think James says his mom didn't really understand art? Do you think James feels his father understands art? (Yes.) Why? (James says the stuff was a lot like what Dad had back home.) Enjoy the page about Warhol's wigs! Read the next page. Ask: What do you think is one of the most important thing the author learned from his uncle? (His uncle made him want to work on his own art when he got home.) Read to the end of the book.

FOLLOW-UP DISCUSSION: How do you think James felt when he found the surprise from Uncle Andy? Why do you think James feels his mom finally understands what art is all about? (She doesn't make him clean up his art studio in his room, and she wakes him up early and drives him to art class on Saturdays.) James says that he learned that art is all around us. What do you think he meant by that? Look at more examples of pop art. Collect recyclables. Create a junkyard of your own. Have children create works of art and then paint a picture of them!

Refer to THE STORY OF FROG BELLY RAT BONE, by Timothy Basil Ering (Candlewick) and STUART'S CAPE, written by Sara Pennypacker and illustrated by Martin Matje (Orchard), in which junk plays a part. See the read-aloud plans found elsewhere in this part of this book.

For additional books about art and artists, refer to Book Notes and Tips and Techniques for Teachers and Librarians.

Notes:

Title	SARAH MORTON'S DAY: A DAY IN THE LIFE OF A PILGRIM GIRL
Author	Kate Winters
Photographer	Russ Kendall
Publisher	Scholastic
Copyright Date	1989
Ages	7 and up
Read-Aloud Time	8–10 minutes
Subject	Pilgrim life in New England in the 1600s

Note: Like to bake? Consider making a batch of cornbread for the children to sample following the reading of the book. Use your own recipe or the one found on the bag of cornmeal. The author suggests not making Indian Corn Bread from the recipe she gives in the book!

This book is one of a set of three that leads the learner through a day in the life of a Pilgrim child. The titles of the others are listed below. This book is illustrated with photographs taken at Plimouth Plantation on Cape Cod, a living outdoor museum that replicates Plymouth in 1627. At this point in history the settlers have lived in religious freedom for seven years in the New World. Interpreters at Plimouth Plantation dress in the garments of the time; complete their chores; and work in their homes, fields, and gardens while conversing with visitors in the language of the time.

PREREADING FOCUS: Show children a map of New England and locate Plymouth. Discuss the time in which the story takes place. Develop an understanding of the reason the Pilgrims sailed to America from Europe. Trace their path on a map. Ask the children to cite facts they know about Pilgrims and their experiences and beliefs. List them on chart paper.

WHILE READING: Show the children the photographs as you read the simple text. Ask children to define words used in context, such as *thee, cockerel, overgarments, perchance, save, muck, gotten the rod, pottage, knicker box, Sabbath,* and *poppet.* There is a glossary at the back of the book.

FOLLOW-UP DISCUSSION: Note interesting facts the children learned from the book on chart paper. Ask the children which parts of Sarah's life they liked and which they didn't. Discuss.

Companions books are SAMUEL EATON'S DAY: A DAY IN THE LIFE OF A PILGRIM BOY and ON THE MAYFLOWER: VOYAGE OF THE SHIP'S APPRENTICE & A PASSENGER GIRL, both written by Kate Waters and illustrated by Russ Kendall (Scholastic).

For a warm and witty look at a Thanksgiving that could have been a disaster but wasn't, see the read-aloud plan for THANKSGIVING AT THE TAPPLETONS, written by Eileen Spinelli and illustrated by Maryann Cocca-Leffler (HarperCollins), found elsewhere in this book.

For more titles on Thanksgiving, refer to Book Notes.

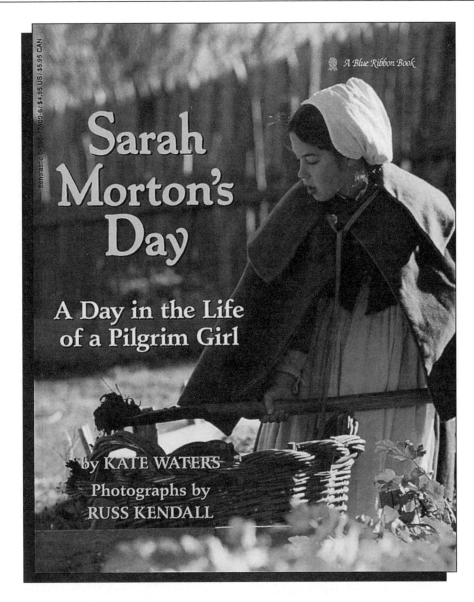

Photograph by Russ Kendall from SARAH MORTON'S DAY: A DAY IN THE
LIFE OF A PILGRIM GIRL by Kate Waters. Photograph copyright © 1989
by Russell Kendall. Used by permission of Scholastic Inc.

Notes:

Title	MY LUCKY DAY
Author/Illustrator	Keiko Kasza
Publisher	Putnam
Copyright Date	2003
Ages	6 and up
Read-Aloud Time	7–10 minutes
Subject	Tale, sly wit

Be sure not to miss a single detail in the spry gouache illustrations that accompany this lively tale of a piglet that outfoxes a fox. On the first full spread, for example, the fox is looking toward the front door where someone is knocking, in search of Rabbit. On the table before Mr. Fox is tooth sharpener, claw polish, and a book opened to a page which reads "Hunting A–Z". On the wall behind him are photos of Fox with his unfortunate quarry. His facial expression immediately clues us in to the kind of character Mr. Fox is. Turn the page to see the facial expression of piglet when Fox opens the door. "Oh, no!" he screams. "Oh, yes!" cries the fox. "You've come to the right place." And you have if you want a tale of sly wit and smart moves with all the trimmings. A pig roast ahead? Don't set your table just yet, my friend. Perhaps you should fatten up that piglet first . . . .

PREREADING FOCUS: Ask: What would happen if a piglet was looking for his friend, Rabbit, and knocked on a fox's door by mistake? If you were the piglet what would you do? **Let's read to find out** what this piglet does and why this book is called MY LUCKY DAY.

WHILE READING: Read the first two pages. Note the details in the illustrations. Ask: Who do you think is at the door? (Piglet.) Show the illustration on the next page. Then read the text here and on the next page. Ask: Whose lucky day is it? (Fox's.) Do you think the piglet would call it a lucky day? (No.) What do you think he will do? Read the next page. Ask: Do you think the fox ought to wash the piglet? Read on, making predictions. Note details in the illustrations. When you get to the page on which the tired fox is giving the piglet a massage, ask: How is Mr. Fox feeling? (Tired!) Turn the page. Ask: What's happened? (Mr. Fox fell asleep!) Read the next page. Ask: So who do you think has had a lucky day after all? (Piglet.) Read the next page. Show the address book and read the entries. Ask: What can you tell me about this piglet? (He planned the whole thing!) Be sure to turn to the last illustration!

FOLLOW-UP DISCUSSION: Ask: Whose lucky day did it turn out to be? (Piglet's.) What do you think will happen at the bear's house? (The piglet will outsmart the bear as he did the fox.) Ask the children to draw pictures of what the piglet might trick the bear into doing.

For another outstanding tale, see the read-aloud plan for CLEVER BEATRICE, written by Margaret Willey and illustrated by Heather Solomon (Atheneum). See Book Notes for additional folk tales, legends, fairy tales, and fractured fairy tales.

Notes:

Title . . . . THE ONE IN THE MIDDLE IS THE GREEN KANGAROO
Author . . . . Judy Blume
Illustrator . . . . Amy Aitken
Publisher . . . . Bradbury
Copyright Date 1981
Ages . . . . 7 and up
Read-Aloud Time . . . . 5–7 minutes; 3 days
Subject . . . . Middle child, school play, confidence, self-image

Second-grader Freddy Dissel is the middle child. He feels "like the peanut butter part of the sandwich, squeezed between Mike and Ellen." He has to wear Mike's hand-me-down clothes, and he had to give up his room and move in with Mike when El-len came along. But all that doesn't matter anymore once Freddy gets the part of the green kangaroo in the fifth- and sixth-grade play. His lines are easy, his stomach is still, and he gets to jump high and low all over the stage. Best of all for Freddy, it's just him all by himself who takes a long, deep bow at the end of the play, at the end of this simple, reassuring short chapter book.

> **PREREADING FOCUS:** *Introducing the book:* Ask: Who has older and younger sis-ters or brothers? Discuss the advantages and disadvantages of being in the middle. Discuss the ups and downs of being the oldest, youngest, or only child in the family. Today we are going to begin a book in four chapters about sec-ond-grader Freddy Dissel, who is in the middle in his family between Mike and Ellen. **Let's read to find out** how he feels about that.

> **WHILE READING:** Read a chapter a day. (On the third day, read chapters 3 and 4, since chapter 4 is a single page.) Each day before you begin, recap briefly what happened in the previous chapter.

Day One: Chapter 1

> *Follow-up:* Who is the main character in this story? Who are the other characters we have met so far in this book? List on chart paper as responses are given. Elicit the characters' relationship to the main character. (Freddy Dissel; Mike—older brother; Ellen—younger sister; Mom.) Reread the first sentence. Ask: What are Freddy's two problems? (Mike and Ellen.) How does being in the middle make Freddy feel? (Like the peanut butter squeezed between two slices of bread.) What are some of the things that bother Freddy about being in the middle? (Sharing clothes, giving up his room to Ellen, can't play with older brother, doesn't enjoy playing with Ellen, getting reprimanded by mom for tak-ing his frustration out on Ellen.) What words would you use to describe how Freddy feels?

Day Two: Chapter 2

Prereading: Ask: What do we know about Freddy? (Use chart paper from yesterday as a prompt.) **Let's read to find out** what happens when Freddy hears about the school play.

Follow-up: Ask: Has Mike ever been in a school play? (No.) Has Ellen ever been in a school play? (No.) Why do you think Freddy waited two whole days before he told Mrs. Gumbler he wanted to be in the school play? (He needed to get up the courage to act.) How does Freddy feel when Mrs. Gumbler says the play is only for fifth and sixth graders? (Disappointed.) Why do you think Freddy felt small when he was up on stage? (Auditorium and stage are big.) Have you ever been on stage? What is it like? Did you feel small? Why do you think Freddy got the part? (He yelled loudly from the stage and he was a great jumper!) How does Freddy feel about getting the part of the green kangaroo? (Great!) Do you think it will be hard to be a second grader in a fifth- and sixth—grade play? How do you know? (He waits to announce it at dinner.) What does he like most about being the green kangaroo? (Just him all by himself, the only one in the play.) What do Mike and Ellen think? (Ellen is giggly and happy; Mike is a bit amazed, maybe a bit envious.) How do Mom and Dad feel about it? (Proud and happy.) How do you know? (Mom kisses him; Dad and Mom praise him.) How do you think things will go for Freddy in the play? In the next chapter Freddy practices his part. What would you practice if you had a part as a kangaroo? Let's practice being Freddy, the green kangaroo! If there is a stage in your school, take kids there on a mini field trip so they can experience what it is like to be on stage.

Day Three: Chapters 3 and 4

Prereading: Review kangaroo practice! If you visited the stage, talk about what it felt like to be on stage. Tell children that today we are going to read about how Freddy practiced for two weeks, and all about the play. **Let's read to find out** how the play turns out.

Follow-up: Ask: What did Freddy do to get ready for the play? (He practiced at home and school; he practiced kangaroo jumps and faces.) What does "Break a leg" mean? (Good luck.) How does Freddy feel just before the play begins? (Scared; nervous.) How do you know? (He couldn't smile; his heart beat fast; his stomach bounced; he felt funny.) Once Freddy got on stage he relaxed. Why? (He had a job to do. He was the only kangaroo!) How do you think Freddy felt at the end of the play? How did he feel at the end of the book? (Glad to be Freddy Dissel.)

For another book by this author about sibling rivalry suitable for this age group, see the picture book THE PAIN AND THE GREAT ONE, illustrated by Irene Trivas (Bradbury), in which the story is told from the points of view of both the older sister and the younger brother.

For another book about a school play, see the read-aloud plan for AMAZING GRACE, written by Mary Hoffman and illustrated by Caroline Binch (Dial) found elsewhere in this part of this book.

For additional titles about family, see Book Notes.

Title	. . . . THE TENTH GOOD THING ABOUT BARNEY
Author	. . . . Judith Viorst
Illustrator	. . . . Erik Blegvad
Publisher	. . . . Atheneum
Copyright Date	 1971
Ages	. . . . 6 and up
Read-Aloud Time	. . . . 5–7 minutes
Subject	. . . . Death of a pet

This is a sweet and simple story about the 10 good things a little boy names about his much loved and sorely missed cat, Barney. As a cat lover who has buried more than one of her buddies in the garden over the years, I can tell you this touching book has a special place on my bookshelf.

PREREADING FOCUS: This may be a book you choose to read one-on-one with a child who has lost a pet. Begin the session by talking about why pets are special. Offer favorite memories you have of moments shared with your pets over the years. Share your regrets for the child's loss. Tell the child that you have a special book you want to read together.

WHILE READING: Read through page 5. Ask: What is a *funeral?* Read page 6. Ask: What do you think he will say about Barney? Read through page 9. Ask: Do you know any cat songs? Read through page 19. Ask: Do you think it was good for him to help his dad in the garden? Why? Read to the end of the book. Ask: How do you think the boy feels at the end of the story? (Better.) Why? (He thinks Barney has a pretty good job in the garden.)

FOLLOW-UP DISCUSSION: Ask: Do you think you could name 10 good things about your pet? Write them down as the child says them or have him write them and then illustrate with a picture of his pet.

For another title on the loss of a pet, this time a dog, see I'LL ALWAYS LOVE YOU, by Hans Wilhelm (Crown).

For additional titles on the topic of death, see Book Notes and Parent Pull-Out Pages.

Notes:

Title . . . . ABRAHAM LINCOLN	
Author . . . . Amy L. Cohn and Suzy Schmidt	
Illustrator . . . . David A. Johnson	
Publisher . . . . Scholastic	
Copyright Date 2002	
Ages . . . . 7 and up	
Read-Aloud Time . . . . 10–15 minutes	
Subject . . . . Biography of Abe Lincoln	

Note: Have a map of the United States and chart paper handy for use during the reading of this biography.

In a perky style, the authors of this biography get down on their haunches to look the primary grade listener in the eye and captivate her with the life story of one of our most beloved and highly honored presidents. With lines such as "all his life his knees and nose got a little too friendly every time he sat down," and "Abe's pants were short, his hands big as shovels," you're sure to keep children riveted to each page of this tall, thin book that no doubt is meant to silhouette the giant inside. A list of important dates in Lincoln's life can be found at the end of the book.

PREREADING FOCUS: Show the back cover of the book. Ask: Who can tell me who this is? (Abraham Lincoln.) What can you tell me about Abraham Lincoln? Flip to the front cover. This is Lincoln as a boy. Tell children that today we are going to read to find out about Abe Lincoln's life, beginning with when he was a baby and going all through his childhood to when he became an adult.

WHILE READING: Read the first page. Find Kentucky on the map. Write down one important fact from the page on the chart paper. Read the next page. Find Indiana on the map. Write down one fact from this page. Read the next page. Discuss what a split-rail fence is, and what it means that it is "horse high, bull strong, pig tight." Read the next page. Ask: What does "figure" mean? (Compute; do math problems.) Why do you think Abe says his name doesn't look like him? (It's short.) Explain what a "yarn" is. (Story.) Define "rithmetic". (Math.) What did we learn Abe likes most to do? (Read.) How do you know? (Eased the pain of his mother's death.) Write three facts from this page on chart paper. Read the next page. Ask: What did Abe mean by saying, "My friend's the one who has a book I ain't read yet"? Write a fact on the chart paper. Read the next page. Trace his flatboat adventure. Read the next page. Find Illinois on the map. Find New Salem. Ask: What do you think "winked out" means? What does "debating" mean? (From context, "convincing others to come around to your way of thinking.") Read the next page. Ask: What is a legislator? (One who makes laws.) Find Springfield on the map. Jot down a fact. Read the next page and note a fact. Read the next two pages. Note a fact. Find Washington, D.C., on the map. Read the next page. Explain, "A house divided against itself cannot stand." Jot down a fact. Read the next three pages. Ask: How did Lincoln keep himself happy during the hard times of war? (Joking, playing with sons.) What was the Emancipation Proclamation? (Declared all slaves free.) List a fact. Read the next two pages. Explain the assassination of Lincoln. Write it down on the chart paper. Read the final page.

FOLLOW-UP DISCUSSION: Review the facts listed on the chart paper. Ask the children which are the most important. Highlight these. Ask them which facts they didn't already know. For an activity to be completed on another day: List the facts in jumbled order on a sheet and reproduce it. Have the children cut out facts and place them in order to make a paragraph about Lincoln's life. More able students may add more details and form their own paragraphs.

For additional biography selections, see Book Notes and Tips and Techniques for Teachers and Librarians.

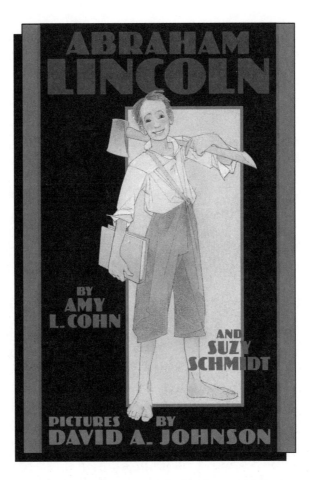

Illustration by David A. Johnson from ABRAHAM LINCOLN by Amy L. Cohn and Suzy Schmidt. Published by Scholastic Press/Scholastic Inc. Illustration © 2002 by David A. Johnson. Used by permission.

Notes:

Title	THE DINOSAURS OF WATERHOUSE HAWKINS
Author	Barbara Kerley
Illustrator	Brian Selznick
Publisher	Scholastic
Copyright Date	2001
Ages	7 and up
Read-Aloud Time	10–15 minutes
Subject	Biography of artist, dinosaurs, believing in yourself, following your dreams

This lush, spectacular specimen of a book highlights the life of artist and sculptor Waterhouse Hawkins, who, in the mid-1800s, showed the world what a dinosaur looked like. Throughout the story Hawkins's energy to pursue his dreams, his belief in himself, and his strength of spirit shine through. Absorbing author and illustrator notes can be found at the back of this Caldecott Honor book.

PREREADING FOCUS: Ask: Can you tell me what a dinosaur looks like? How do you know about dinosaurs? Have you ever seen a real dinosaur? Why not? (They are extinct.) How do you think we learned about dinosaurs if they are extinct? Show the cover of the book. Read the title. Point out the dinosaur being held by Hawkins and the one behind him. Explain that this is an illustration, or picture, of a man who helped people understand dinosaurs and see what they looked like. Ask: What is a *biography*? (A true story about a person's life.) **Let's read to find out** about the life of Waterhouse Hawkins.

WHILE READING: As you read through the book, take time to enjoy the many details in the illustrations. Note the use of color to depict mood. Read the first spread. Ask: What have we learned so far? (Setting is London, 1853; horse-drawn carriages as means of transportation; Waterhouse's first name was Benjamin.) Determine where London is. Ask: Why did the horses *clatter*? (The streets are brick.) Note what surrounds Waterhouse. Ask: Who do you think his important visitors might be? Read the next page. Ask: What is sculpting? (Carving, modeling, or welding materials into works of art.) Read the next page. Why is Waterhouse excited? (He will build dinosaurs for Crystal Palace.) What is a *fossil*? (A remnant or impression of an organism from the past.) How did Hawkins manage to sculpt dinosaurs with only bits and pieces of bone to go by? (He was helped by scientist Richard Owen, "who checked every muscle, bone, and spike.") Read the next page to find out how Waterhouse accomplished his goal. Discuss. Read the next page and note the steps outlined in the illustration. Read the next two pages that detail the dinner party with "style"! Read about the unveiling of the dinosaurs on the next two pages. Ask: How do you think Waterhouse felt at that moment? Show the next spread. Read the next page. Ask: Who has been to Central Park in New York City? Read the next page. Note the "Chapter Two" aspect. Read the next two pages. Ask: How do you think Waterhouse felt about working on American dinosaurs and building such a grand museum? Read the next page. Ask: Do you think it took courage for Waterhouse to speak out against "Boss"? Read the next page. Ask: How does Waterhouse feel now? What do you think he will do? Why do you think the artist of this book made this page brown? (To depict the sense of defeat Waterhouse felt.) Study the next spread. Read the next two pages. What do we know about Waterhouse's spirit that he could go on after such a setback to continue to teach and bring dinosaurs to life for Americans? Turn the page to "Chapter 3" and ask why this would be a "new chapter". (Waterhouse returned home.) Read to the end. Be sure to share the illustration on the last page.

FOLLOW-UP DISCUSSION: Review the facts learned. Discuss Waterhouse Hawkins's spirit and how it helped him to accomplish great things in his life. Ask: Do you know anyone else in history or alive today who has a great spirit and has accomplished great things?

For additional books on dinosaurs and the arts, refer to Book Notes.

For other notable biographies, see Tips and Techniques for Teachers and Librarians and Book Notes.

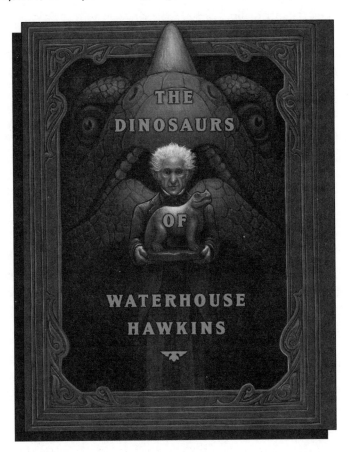

Illustration by Brian Selznick from THE DINOSAURS OF WATERHOUSE HAWKINS by Barbara Kerley. Published by Scholastic Press/Scholastic Inc. Illustration copyright © 2001 by Brian Selznick. Used by permission.

Title	ME ON THE MAP
Author	Joan Sweeney
Illustrator	Annette Cole
Publisher	Crown
Copyright Date	1996
Ages	5 and up
Read-Aloud Time	6–8 minutes
Subject	Geography, introduction to map skills, a sense of place

Note: Collect a variety of maps to share with children following the reading of the book. See notes in Follow-up Discussion.

From "me," to my town, to the world laid flat, this simple book introduces children to maps and a sense of place. Brightly illustrated with clear, uncluttered, realistic drawings, this book features a little girl who speaks to the reader and introduces the concept in an unintimidating and most appealing way. She begins with "This is me," then moves to a map of her room, her home, her town, her state, the country, and the world. From there she works backward to end up back in her familiar space—her bedroom. A perfect pick to launch a study of geography or a unit on the different regions of our country or world.

PREREADING FOCUS: Ask: How would you find your way somewhere if you didn't know how to get there? (Use a map.) What is a map? Has your mom or dad ever used a map? Discuss. What other maps can you think of? (World maps, building maps, state maps.) **Let's read to find out** more about maps.

WHILE READING: As you read through the book, study the maps provided. Note the details on the various maps pictured here. Ask the children to come up with reasons why we need maps of various places.

FOLLOW-UP DISCUSSION: Review the different kinds of maps the narrator showed us. Present other examples of maps not shown in the book, such as a globe, natural resource map, fire exit map, or car map. Ask the children to make a map of their choice. Possibilities include a map of the classroom, the school, the playground, or their room in their home. Display.

For books on different places in our world, look for the Caldecott Honor and Reading Rainbow selection, WHEN I WAS YOUNG IN THE MOUNTAINS, written by Cynthia Rylant and illustrated by Diane Goode (Dutton), and the classic, MISS RUMPHIUS, by Barbara Cooney (Viking).

For additional titles, refer to Book Notes.

Notes:

Title	CATWINGS
Author	Ursula K. LeGuin
Illustrator	S. D. Schindler
Publisher	Orchard
Copyright Date	1988
Ages	7 and up
Read-Aloud Time	8–10 minutes per chapter; 4 chapters
Subject	Fantasy, cats, family

This slim fantasy is an American Bookseller Pick of the List by an author known and loved among readers of all ages and one who is sure to captivate your audience. From the cats cavorting on the endpapers to the final chapter, you'll be transported from the city dump to good Hands. Enjoy.

PREREADING FOCUS: *Introducing the book:* Ask: Who has a cat? What do cats like to do? How do they act? Discuss. Ask: Can cats fly? Can they talk? Today we are going to begin reading a *fantasy*, or an imaginary tale. It is about cats that have wings. Show the cover of the book. Like many fantasies, there are aspects of the story that could be true. Discuss the elements of well-known fantasies they may have read.

WHILE READING: Read a chapter a day. Note cat behaviors that are realistic and those that are not. Develop an understanding of the elements of fantasy. Each day before you begin reading, recap briefly what happened in the previous chapter.

Note preparations for Day 3.

Day One: Chapter 1

Follow-up: List the characters. Ask: Why is the neighborhood unsafe? What has Mrs. Jane Tabby taught her children? What is another name for a striped cat? (Tabby.) Why did Mrs. Jane Tabby send her children off? What do you think will happen next?

Day Two: Chapter 2

Prereading: Ask: What has taken place so far in this story? **Let's read to find out** what happens to Thelma, Roger, James, and Harriet now that they are on their own in the world.

Follow-up: Ask: Why do the cats have difficulty flying? (They are plump. They don't have the knack for gliding yet.) What new experiences do they have in this chapter? (The smell of factories; night flying; the differences they find in the country.) Why did the cats think the country was a much better place than the city? What might be some dangers in the country?

Day Three: Chapter 3

Prereading: Review chapter 2. Ask: What do you think will happen to the cats in the country? **Let's read to find out.**

While Reading: Read the first section of the chapter. Ask: Why are the birds outraged? (The cats can fly!) Why are they afraid? (The cats can reach their young in the nests.) What can the birds do better than the cats? (Fly; don't get tangled up in trees; don't bump into trees; speed up and do fancy maneuvers when flying.) What does the storyteller mean when she says, "Owl is not a quick thinker. She is a long thinker"? What are *talons*? What do you think Owl will do? Let's keep reading the chapter to find out.

Follow-up: Ask: What did the cats learn from being attacked by Owl? (How birds feel when they are attacked by cats.) Why was the owl gone in the morning? (Owls are *nocturnal.* They are active at night.) Why does the country sound like the old neighborhood? (Noisy.) What does Harriet mean by *Shoes*? (People.) What does Roger mean by the *Hands*? (People who picked up the cats when they were kittens.) What are the "right kind of Hands"? Why does Harriet think she's found the right kind of Hands? (Because of the way the person behaved.) Discuss. Who do you think might be the Hands? How do you picture this person? What do you think will happen next? Pass out copies of the lines of characters from the opening scene of this chapter (p. 19–top of p. 20) and pages 26–30. Highlight different characters' lines in different colors. Assign parts to able readers and re-read the dialogue. Act as narrator. Encourage expression!

Day Four: Chapter 4

Prereading: Review what the Tabbys have learned. How do we know they are growing up? (They are sounding more and more like their mother.) **Let's read to find out** what happens the next day and who the Hands belong to.

Follow-up: Ask: Who are the Hands? (Susan and Hank.) How do the Hands win over the cats? (They don't scare them off.) Why do the cats trust the Hands? (They are kind and patient. They let the cats come to them. They develop trust.) What do you think will happen next? Tell children about the sequels (show covers if available) and encourage them to read them on their own or to read them with a parent. Send home a list of the CATWINGS titles with bibliographic information.

Additional titles in the series include CATWINGS RETURN, JANE ON HER OWN: A CATWINGS TALE, and WONDERFUL ALEXANDER AND THE CATWINGS.

Title..........................MR. POTTER'S PET
Author........................Dick King-Smith
Illustrator.........................Mark Teague
Publisher...........................Hyperion
Copyright Date.........................1996
Ages...........................7 and up
Read-Aloud Time...........8–10 minutes per chapter
Subject.............Pet birds, growing up, humor

Mr. Potter's pet is an irascible coot that's a hoot. Listeners will be delighted by his irreverent comments, his big heart, and the way he pushes Potter toward happiness. From the English author of BABE: THE GALLANT PIG (from which an award-winning feature film was made) and a host of other fantasies featuring memorable animals, this simple tale illustrated by the master, Teague (see DEAR MRS. LARUE), is an excellent introduction to the worlds he creates in books kids will love and remember.

PREREADING FOCUS: *Introducing the book:* Ask: Have you ever wanted something so much you just couldn't stop thinking about it? Discuss. Who has a pet? Did you always have your pet, or do you remember a time when you really wanted a pet and then you got one? What was that like? Why did you really, really want a pet? Today we are going to begin a book about Mr. Potter, who really, really wants a pet. Show the cover. Ask: What kind of pet do you think Mr. Potter will get? (Bird.) **Let's read to find out**.

WHILE READING: Read a chapter a day. Note how Mr. Potter's pet helps him. Each day before you begin reading, recap briefly what happened in the previous chapter.

*Note preparation below for chapters 1 and 2.

Day One: Chapter 1

While Reading: Read the first page. Ask: What is an *addiction*? (A need for something.) Show the illustration. Ask: What do you think his addiction is? Read the next page through to the end of the chapter.

Follow-up: Ask: Would you have bought that mynah? What do you think he should name him? What do you think will happen next? Show the photograph of a black Indian mynah.

Day Two: Chapter 2

Prereading: Ask: What has taken place so far in this story? **Let's read to find out** what happens when Mr. Potter gets his new pet home.

Follow-up: Ask: Why did Mr. Potter buy this mynah? (It could speak as clearly as any human.) Why do you think Mr. Potter named the mynah Everest? (After the mountain.) What happens at the end of the chapter? (Everest leaves through the open window.) How do you think Mr. Potter feels? What do you think will happen next? Read about mynahs from a reference such as a bird book or the encyclopedia.

*Cover of MR. POTTER'S PET, copyright 1996 by Mark Teague,
reprinted with permission of Hyperion Books for Children.*

Day Three: Chapter 3

Prereading: Review chapter 2. Ask: What do you think will happen in this chapter? **Let's read to find out**.

While Reading: Use expression while reading Everest's cantankerous lines!

Follow-up: Ask: Do you think Everest will fly away again? (No.) Why? (Too cold; too many cats; it's better with Potter.) What has Mr. Potter taught Everest? (Home is good. Where to go to the bathroom.) What do you think will happen next?

Day Four: Chapter 4

Prereading: Review where the last chapter ended. **Let's read to find out** what Mr. Potter does about a housekeeper.

Follow-up: Ask: What sign did Mr. Potter give Everest? (Scratched his bald spot.) Do you think Everest liked the housekeepers? (No.) How do you know? (He obliged Mr. Potter!)

Day Five: Chapter 5

Prereading: Review where the last chapter ended. **Let's read to find out** whether the third time is lucky for Mr. Potter.

Follow-up: Ask: What sign did Mr. Potter give Everest by mistake? (He scratched his head.) Why did Mr. Potter shout "No!" at Everest? (He thought Everest might dismiss Peggy and he didn't want him to do that.) Does Everest like Peggy? (Yes.) How do you know? What do you think will happen next?

Day Six: Chapter 6

Prereading: Review what we know about the new housekeeper. (Mr. Potter's girl-friend from forty years ago. She is kind, plump, and gets along well with Potter and Everest.) Do you think she will make a good housekeeper? Why? **Let's read to find out** how things go.

Follow-up: Ask: What does Everest do when he is happy or pleased? (Nibbles on an ear.) Everest is very clever in getting Peggy and Potter together. Review. Ask: What do you think will happen in the final chapter?

Day Seven: Chapter 7

Prereading: In this chapter we learn what Mr. Potter gets for Peggy as a wedding gift. What do you think it is? **Let's read to find out**.

Follow-up: Ask: What do you think the Potters ought to name the new pet? Why is Everest happy? (He has a new friend.) Who is your favorite character in this book? Why?

Other titles by Dick King-Smith include BABE: THE GALLANT PIG, A MOUSE CALLED WOLF, MARTIN'S MICE, and THREE TERRIBLE TRINS.

Notes:

Tips and Techniques for
Teachers and Librarians

Reading Aloud to Beginning Readers

PART 1: PICTURE BOOKS

Horror stories abound:

Once children learn to recognize their numbers and letters and graduate from kindergarten, there's no need or time for picture books.

Parents don't want teachers to read picture books to their first graders. Spend time reading REAL books! Bring on those BIG KID books!

Older children don't want to see or hear picture books. They're for babies.

A publisher's Web site suggests it's time for chapter books once children sport a kindergarten graduation cap.

Hogwash.

You're never too old for a thoughtfully illustrated, well-written picture book. And you're certainly not too old in first or second grade. So relax, sit back, and take the time to smell the roses you swear have a scent in that glossy oversized book you hold up for all to see. Your test scores will prove your wisdom in not leaving behind these tomes of pleasure. These are the books that will endear children to reading, and the more they like it, the more they'll do it. These are the books they'll remember as adults. Don't you? These are the books that form the foundation for lifelong reading habits.

To further salve your guilty conscience, keep in mind that picture books vary dramatically in length, depth, and treatment of subject matter. For every picture book under 200 words you can find one with full-page text facing full-color art. For every wordless chunky book made for teethers, there is a picture storybook that features a main character, a memorable setting, a plot with a conflict, and a satisfying resolution. Picture books offer story, facts, and memories. Make the most of them. Think how hard it is for your colleagues down the hall to justify reading picture books to those BIG third graders. Heck, they're almost out the door on their way to middle school! (That's not a growth; that's my tongue in my cheek.)

Choose books randomly to read aloud as a way to begin the day, to rally the troops before lunch, and after lunch to ease the transition from the cafeteria to academic afternoon activities. These choices may be seasonal, funny, reflective, or simply a favorite of yours.

Choose a picture book to launch a class project, enhance a unit of study, or illustrate a point you wish to make (No pun intended!). Following are some examples to get you thinking along the lines of extending teachable moments or cementing concepts or classroom values using picture books as a small part or the crux of a unit of study.

Writing

Want to drive home the importance of being able to write a letter, to correspond and connect in writing? Flip to the read-aloud plans for

- CLICK, CLACK, MOO, COWS THAT TYPE, written by Doreen Cronin and illustrated by Betsy Lewin (Simon & Schuster)

- DEAR MRS. LARUE: LETTERS FROM OBEDIENCE SCHOOL, by Mark Teague (Scholastic)

- PUNCTUATION TAKES A VACATION, written by Robin Pulver and illustrated by Lynn Rowe Reed (Holiday House)

See also

- ANGELINA BALLERINA'S INVITATION TO THE BALLET, written by Katharine Holabird and illustrated by Helen Craig (Pleasant Company)

- THE JOLLY POSTMAN OR OTHER PEOPLE'S LETTERS, by Janet and Allan Ahlberg (Little, Brown)

- THE JOLLY POCKET POSTMAN, by Janet Ahlberg and Allan Ahlberg (Little Brown)

- THE JOLLY CHRISTMAS POSTMAN, by Janet Ahlberg and Allan Ahlberg (Little Brown)

- DEAR ANNIE, by Judith Caseley (Greenwillow)

- BEETHOVEN LIVES UPSTAIRS, written by Barbara Nichol and illustrated by Scott Cameron (Orchard Books)

- FREDERICK, by Leo Lionni (Random House)

- THE GARDENER, written by Sarah Stewart and illustrated by David Small (Farrar, Straus & Giroux)

Biography

Notable biographies for this age group include

- UNCLE ANDY'S, by James Warhola (Putnam); about Andy Warhol. See the read-aloud plan.

- THE DINOSAURS OF WATERHOUSE HAWKINS, written by Barbara Kerley and illustrated by Brian Selznick (Scholastic); a Caldecott Honor book. See the read-aloud plan.

- ACTION JACKSON, written by Jan Greenberg and Sandra Jordan and illustrated by Robert Andrew Parker (Roaring Brook Press); a Robert F. Sibert Honor Book; about Jackson Pollock.

- SO YOU WANT TO BE PRESIDENT?, written by Judith St. George and illustrated by David Small (Philomel); short, humorous anecdotes about each of our past presidents through Bill Clinton; winner of the Caldecott Medal.

- SO YOU WANT TO BE AN INVENTOR?, written by Judith St. George and illustrated by David Small (Philomel); in the style of the previous book.

- THE POT THAT JUAN BUILT, written by Nancy Andrews-Goebel and illustrated by David Diaz (Lee & Low Books); about Juan Quezada, "premier potter in Mexico."

- HENRY HIKES TO FITCHBURG and HENRY BUILDS A CABIN, by D. B. Johnson (Houghton Mifflin); intriguing facets of Henry David Thoreau's life.

- TO FLY: THE STORY OF THE WRIGHT BROTHERS, written by Wendie C. Old and illustrated by Robert Andrew Parker (Clarion).

- MARY SMITH, by A. U'Ren (Farrar, Straus & Giroux); the story of knocker-up Mary Smith, who in the 1920s, before alarm clocks were widely used, shot dried peas from a rubber tube at the windows of her clients in London to wake them for work.

- PLAYERS IN PIGTAILS, written by Shana Corey and illustrated by Rebecca Gibbon (Scholastic); a fictional tale based on facts about a young woman who played in the All-American Girls Professional Baseball League during World War II.

- ABRAHAM LINCOLN, written by Amy L. Cohn and Suzy Schmidt and illustrated by David A. Johnson (Scholastic). See the read-aloud plan.

*Illustration by Rebecca Gibbon from PLAYERS IN PIGTAILS by Shana Corey.
Published by Scholastic Press/Scholastic Inc. Illustration copyright
© 2003 by Rebecca Gibbon. Used by permission.*

Want to examine black history? Begin with

- MARTIN'S BIG WORDS: THE LIFE OF MARTIN LUTHER KING, JR., written by Doreen Rappaport and illustrated by Bryan Collier (Hyperion). See the read-aloud plan.

Move on to

- FLY HIGH! THE STORY OF BESSIE COLEMAN, written by Louise Borden and Mary Kay Kroeger and illustrated by Teresa Flavin (McElderry Books).

- WHEN MARIAN SANG, written by Pam Munoz Ryan and illustrated by Brian Selznick (Scholastic); a Robert F. Sibert Honor Book; about Marian Anderson's rise to fame in the 1930s.

- GOIN' SOMEPLACE SPECIAL, written by Patricia C. McKissack and illustrated by Jerry Pinkney (Atheneum); finding acceptance at the public library in pre-civil rights era.

Martin Luther King Jr.'s contributions were never easier to access, and true accounts such as these debunk the theory that facts are dry and history doesn't engage young readers and listeners.

Values; Character Education

Have a bully in your midst? Reach for

- STAND TALL, MOLLY LOU MELON, written by Patty Lovell and illustrated by David Catrow (Putnam). See the read-aloud plan.

- COCK-A-DOODLE-DUDLEY, by Bill Peet (Houghton Mifflin). See the read-aloud plan.

Other choices to open discussions include

- TYRONE THE HORRIBLE, by Hans Wilhelm (Scholastic).

- TYRONE THE DOUBLE DIRTY ROTTEN CHEATER, by Hans Wilhelm (Scholastic).

- THE RECESS QUEEN, written by Alexis O'Neill and illustrated by Laura Huliska-Beith (Scholastic).

- LOUD-MOUTHED GEORGE AND THE SIXTH-GRADE BULLY, by Nancy Carlson (Carolrhoda).

- BULLY TROUBLE, written by Joanna Cole and illustrated by Marylin Hafner (Random House) (Step into Reading, Step 2).

- SWEET BRIAR GOES TO SCHOOL, written by Karma Wilson and illustrated by LeUyen Pham (Dial).

- DOG EARED, by Amanda Harvey (Doubleday).

Need to discuss manners with the group? From citizenship and respect to burping, there's a picture book sure to tickle—and teach—those little rascals:

- WE LIVE HERE TOO! KIDS TALK ABOUT GOOD CITIZENSHIP, written by Nancy Loewen and illustrated by Omarr Wesley (Picture Window Books).

- IT'S A SPOON, NOT A SHOVEL, written by Caralyn Buehner and illustrated by Mark Buehner (Puffin). See also I DID IT, I'M SORRY, by the same author and illustrator.

- EXCUSE ME!, by Lisa Kopelke (Simon & Schuster).

- MANNERS, by Aliki (HarperCollins); See also COMMUNICATION, by the same author/illustrator.

- PERFECT PIGS, written by Marc Brown and illustrated by Stephen Krensky (Little, Brown).

- THE ANT AND THE ELEPHANT, by Bill Peet (Houghton Mifflin). See the read-aloud plan.

- MY DOG NEVER SAYS PLEASE, written by Suzanne Williams and illustrated by Tedd Arnold (Penguin).

- CHICKEN SUNDAY, by Patricia Polacco (Philomel).

Culminate curricular study with a picture book related to the theme of the unit. When you need to get the message across effectively, reach for the perfect picture book. When the class needs a laugh, a picture book can lighten the load. Fiction and nonfiction picture books abound, and they're guaranteed to make classroom study lively and accessible. And because well-executed picture books engage multiple senses, they make the subject memorable. It's a win-win situation. So sit back, feast your eyes, and smell the roses!

Refer to Book Notes for hundreds of books listed by subject and briefly described that are suitable for six- to eight-year-olds.

Reading Aloud to Beginning Readers

PART 2: BEGINNING READER BOOKS

In the read-aloud portion of this resource you will find selected early chapter books highlighted. These titles particularly lend themselves to being read aloud and offer a practical way to introduce a series of books about a character your listeners are certain to love. Pique their interest with one title and then let them loose to get to know the character better as they read the sequels on their own! Others are listed below under the heading "Begin with One . . . ".

Bridging the important transition from listening to picture books to reading full-bodied chapter books independently are beginning reader books, which target five- to eight-year-old readers. The levels are labeled clearly on the cover or spine for the convenience of teachers and parents. Often included is a page of simple pointers or advice for adults who are purchasing the book.

Pick up any children's publisher's catalog or educational resource catalog, or go to any bookstore, and you'll find an amazing array of beginning readers. Often published in paperback, these slim volumes, typically 48 pages in length, are colorful, smaller in size and heft than most hardcover picture books, and relatively inexpensive. They're written in a simple, structured style in a short chapter format. Meant to hook newly independent readers, they're attractively packaged, the print is large, and there's lots of white space surrounding the text. Illustrations are smaller, less frequent, and less dramatic than those found in picture books. Often they are black-and-white line drawings meant to provide a backdrop for the story. Nevertheless, the illustrations aid in comprehension. While they are not central to the story as they are in picture books, they do enhance meaning. Most important, they give the book an older, more sophisticated feel.

In this established genre, some classics are 40 years old or more! Series are debuted often and new titles released regularly. Listed below are some of the best beginning readers, with a short blurb about each. They are ideal for youngsters reading on a first- or second-grade level to read independently.

A teacher can best match a book to his or her individual students' reading levels. Fortunately, the plethora of inexpensive beginning reader titles available makes "real" books accessible and the connection truly rewarding when the right book is placed in a child's hands at the right time. Happy hunting! Merry matching-making!

Hello Reader!: These single-title books make up a library of their own. Published by Scholastic, there are four levels from preschool through grade 3. Over the years many authors and illustrators have contributed to this line, and a bounty of subjects are covered. A brief note to "family members" about how to encourage beginning readers is found at the front of each book. Favorite titles for grades 1–2 include

THAT FAT HAT, written by Joanne Barkan and illustrated by Maggie Swanson; BUBBLE TROUBLE, written by Mary Packard and illustrated by Elena Kucharik; TWO CRAZY PIGS, written by Karen Berman Nagel and illustrated by Brian Schatell; WAKE ME IN SPRING, written by James Preller and illustrated by Jeffrey Scherer; MORE SPAGHETTI, I SAY!, written by Rita Golden Gelman and illustrated by Jack Kent; FOOTPRINTS IN THE SNOW, written by Cynthia Benjamin and illustrated by Jacqueline Rogers; FALL LEAVES, written by Mary Packard and illustrated by Dana Regan; THE POPCORN SHOP, written by Alice Low and illustrated by Patti Hammel; ALL TUTUS SHOULD BE PINK, written by Sheri Brownrigg and illustrated by Meredith Johnson; BONY-LEGS, written by Joanna Cole and illustrated by Dirk Zimmer; and the I AM . . . Hello Reader! Science titles, written by Jean Marzollo (of I SPY fame) and illustrated by Judith Moffatt. *Note:* Scholastic is no longer publishing new titles in this line.

Rookie Readers: These easy-to-manage, slim, square readers are published by Children's Press and offer simple text and appealing drawings. They are emergent reader-friendly in every aspect. Favorite titles include JOSHUA JAMES LIKES TRUCKS, written by Catherine Petrie and illustrated by Jerry Warshaw; WAIT, SKATES!, written by Mildred D. Johnson and illustrated by Tom Dunnington; SHINE, SUN!, written by Carol Greene and illustrated by Gene Sharp; DIRTY LARRY, written by Bobbie Hamsa and illustrated by Paul Sharp; and MICE!, written by Julie E. Frankel and illustrated by Mike Venezia.

I Can Read It All By Myself Beginner Books: Published by Random House, these books, many of which were written by Dr. Seuss, comprise titles you most likely knew as a child. Classics by Seuss include THE CAT IN THE HAT, HOP ON POP, THE FOOT BOOK, and GREEN EGGS AND HAM. Other titles are GO, DOG, GO! and ARE YOU MY MOTHER? (by P. D. Eastman). A read-aloud plan for GREEN EGGS AND HAM can be found in the Pre-K–K level volume of the Children's Book Corner series.

Step Into Reading: Published by Random House, there are four levels in this series, which, similar to other publishers' series, offers a variety of books on myriad subjects with a note to parents at the front of the book. Step 2 is for grades 1–3 and includes such notable titles as BABAR AND THE GHOST: AN EASY-TO-READ VERSION, by Laurent De Brunhoff; and HUNGRY, HUNGRY SHARKS (illustrated by Patricia Wynne) and BULLY TROUBLE (illustrated by Marylin Hafner), both written by Joanna Cole, the famed author of The Magic School Bus series (Scholastic).

I Can Read Books: This recently redesigned and repackaged series by HarperCollins boasts five levels, from MY FIRST Shared Reading, designated for preschool, to Advanced Reading 4, simple chapter books for grades 3 and up. Authors, illustrators, and topics vary, and over 60 million copies have been sold since 1957. Classics such as FROG AND TOAD, AMELIA BEDELIA, DANNY AND THE DINOSAUR, and LITTLE BEAR are highlighted below. Other must-not-miss titles for grades 1–2 include WHAT DO YOU HEAR WHEN COWS SING? AND OTHER SILLY RIDDLES, by Marco and Giulio Maestro; BLAST OFF! POEMS

ABOUT SPACE, selected by Lee Bennett Hopkins and illustrated by Melissa Sweet; CLARA AND THE BOOKWAGON, written by Nancy Smiler Levinson and illustrated by Carolyn Croll; THE GRANDMA MIX-UP, by award-winning Emily Arnold McCully; NO MORE MONSTERS FOR ME!, written by Peggy Parish (author of AMELIA BEDELIA) and illustrated by Marc Simont; AND I MEANT IT, STANLEY, by Crosby Bonsall; and SCRUFFY, written by Peggy Parish and illustrated by Kelly Oeschsli. See also The High-Rise Private Eyes Series by Cynthia Rylant, highlighted below.

Let's-Read-and-Find-Out Science: Listed as one of the top 10 nonfiction series by the American Library Association, these leveled books published by HarperCollins present science concepts in a colorful, engaging manner. Stage 2 books are meant for children in the primary grades. Representative titles include SPINNING SPIDERS, written by Melvin Berger and illustrated by S. D. Schindler; DOLPHIN TALK: WHISTLES, CLICKS, AND CLAPPING JAWS, written by Wendy Pfeffer and illustrated by Helen K. Davie; and GERMS MAKE ME SICK!, written by Melvin Berger and illustrated by Marylin Hafner.

Frog and Toad Books: Award-winning Arnold Lobel is the author/illustrator of these HarperCollins I Can Read Books (DAYS WITH FROG AND TOAD; FROG AND TOAD ALL YEAR; FROG AND TOAD ARE FRIENDS) as well as GRASSHOPPER ON THE ROAD. Absolute favorites among teachers and new readers alike, these classics from the 1970s continue to delight and develop skills in beginning readers. Pure fun.

MOUSE SOUP; MOUSE TALES: Also written and illustrated by Arnold Lobel and published by HarperCollins, these classics feature mice. MOUSE SOUP relates in a series of chapters how a mouse uses story to outwit a weasel who wants to make mouse soup of him. In MOUSE TALES, Papa Mouse has a bedtime tale for each of his seven mice boys.

Oliver and Amanda Pig Books: Written by Jean Van Leeuwen and illustrated by Arnold Lobel, these books are part of the Puffin Easy-to-Read Program. In the Pig family, Oliver is the older brother to little sister, Amanda. Everyday events become humorous and memorable in these delightful classics.

Morris and Boris Books: This wacky duo—one bear, one moose—could easily have invented slapstick. Their escapades will endear them to beginning readers and have these youngsters begging for more. Written and illustrated by Bernard Wiseman (Penguin).

Little Bear Books: Written by Else Holmelund Minarik and illustrated by Maurice Sendak, titles include LITTLE BEAR, LITTLE BEAR'S VISIT, FATHER BEAR COMES HOME, and LITTLE BEAR'S FRIEND. Part of the HarperCollins I Can Read series, these books are classics that have enthralled generations of beginning readers.

MRS. WISHY-WASHY; WISHY-WASHY DAY: Popular classroom books written by Joy Cowley and illustrated by Elizabeth Fuller and published by The Wright Group. They are certain to engage and delight those just beginning to read on their own.

MILK AND COOKIES: This is one of Frank Asch's "Bear Stories," published in 1982 (Parents Magazine Press), starring the delightful young bear who makes his appearance in many books by Asch dealing with common childhood concerns, from nightmares to birthday parties. Simple text and engaging story lines.

AGAPANTHUS HUM AND THE EYEGLASSES; AGAPANTHUS HUM AND THE ANGEL HOOT: Written by Joy Cowley and illustrated by Jennifer Plecas (Philomel), these charming and humorous chapter books center around "whizzy, dizzy" Agapanthus and her friends; for the advancing first- and second- grade independent reader.

THE STORIES JULIAN TELLS; MORE STORIES JULIAN TELLS: The main character featured in these books, written by Ann Cameron and illustrated by Ann Strugnell (Knopf), likes to tell stories: tall, tall tales that get him into a heap of trouble. Mischievous humor, lots of imagination, and a cast of characters including Dad, little bro Huey, and best friend Gloria; for those reading on the second-grade level. For more books about these characters, see titles about Huey and Gloria as well as additional titles featuring Julian.

Illustration by Jeffrey Scherer from WAKE ME IN SPRING by James Preller. Illustration copyright © 1994 by Jeffrey Scherer. Used by permission of Scholastic Inc.

Illustration by Maggie Swanson from THAT FAT HAT by Joanne Barkan.
A Hello Reader! published by Cartwheel Books/Scholastic Inc.
Illustrations copyright © 1992 by Maggie Swanson. Used by permission.

Series

Hopscotch Hill School Series: This newly launched series of paperback beginning
readers are written by Valerie Tripp and illustrated by Joy Allen. They are published
by Pleasant Company, makers of American Girl products. Beautifully and warmly
illustrated in color throughout, each book offers a story in chapters about one of the
children in Hopscotch Hill School. Also included are a number of "Dear Parents"
notes and activities created by teachers and child specialists who act as advisors

to the series. Related to the theme of each book, these pointers encourage discussion and reinforce the skills and concepts learned in the book in a light and entertaining fashion.

Henry and Mudge Series: Created in 1987, this series written by Cynthia Rylant and illustrated by Sucie Stevenson (and more recently Carolyn Bracken "in the style of Sucie Stevenson") , has won numerous awards and accolades as well as selling millions of copies. Part of Simon & Schuster's Ready-to-Read program, these books will connect young independent readers with the world of Henry and his big dog, Mudge, through short chapters filled with simple, happy sentences.

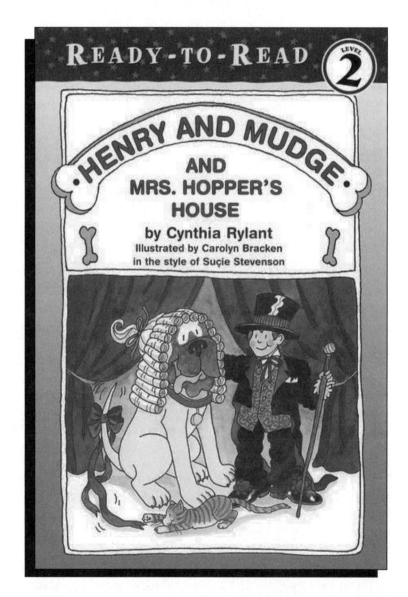

Cover art, text, and illustrations copyright © 2003 HENRY AND MUDGE AND MRS. HOPPER'S HOUSE written by Cynthia Rylant and illustrated by Carolyn Bracken in the style of Suçie Stevenson. Used with permission of Simon & Schuster Books for Young Readers, a division of Simon & Schuster Children's Publishing.

Amelia Bedelia Series: This maid who takes things literally has been delighting readers for 40 years as she turns everyday duties and chores into hilarious mishaps. Most titles are written by Peggy Parish and illustrated by Lynn Sweat. These popular commercial beginning readers (20 million have been sold) are published by Greenwillow/HarperCollins. Since Parish's death in 1988, the series has continued with installments written by Parish's nephew, Herman.

The High-Rise Private Eyes Series: This series is part of the HarperCollins I Can Read Book program, Level 2: Reading with Help. Written by Cynthia Rylant and illustrated by G. Brian Karas, they feature Bunny Brown and Jack Jones. "Bunny is the brains and Jack is the snoop," and they solve simple cases in short and easy chapters, all the while managing to regale the new reader with humorous conversation filled with warmth and wit. Titles include THE CASE OF THE MISSING MONKEY, THE CASE OF THE CLIMBING CAT, and THE CASE OF THE PUZZLING POSSUM.

Horrible Harry Series: Harry is that second-grade kid who keeps things challenging for adults and exciting for kids by dreaming up tons of horrible ideas: and then bringing them to fruition. From showing Song Lee his pet snake and making her squeal to being a dead fish in the Thanksgiving play, Harry will keep kids giggling: and reading. Titles include HORRIBLE HARRY IN ROOM 2B, HORRIBLE HARRY AND THE GREEN SLIME, HORRIBLE HARRY AND THE ANT INVASION, and HORRIBLE HARRY AND THE MUD GREMLINS, written by Suzy Kline and illustrated by Frank Remkiewicz (Viking). For those reading on a second-grade level.

Magic Tree House Series: Published by Random House, these new classics, written by Mary Pope Osborne and illustrated by Sal Murdocca, chronicle the fantastical adventures of Jack and his sister Annie when they climb into a tree house that has appeared mysteriously in the woods near their home. Titles include DINOSAURS BEFORE DARK, MIDNIGHT ON THE MOON, AFTERNOON ON THE AMAZON, PIRATES PAST NOON, and POLARS BEARS PAST BEDTIME. For those on a second-grade reading level.

The Kids of the Polk Street School: A library of titles written by teacher, reading consultant, and award-winning author Patricia Reilly Giff, about the kids in Ms. Rooney's classroom. Heartwarming, reassuring, inviting chapter books for the child reading on a second-grade level; illustrated by Blanche Sims and published by Dell. Other series by the same author include New Kids at the Polk Street School and Polka Dot Private Eye.

Marvin Redpost Series: Written by award-winning author Louis Sachar, these "First Stepping Stone" books published by Random House revolve around the misadventures of a third-grade boy with an imagination that keeps things interesting and funny: a surefire combination to keep young readers begging for more. Titles include MARVIN REDPOST: KIDNAPPED AT BIRTH?; MARVIN REDPOST: WHY PICK ON ME?; MARVIN REDPOST: IS HE A GIRL?; and MARVIN REDPOST: ALONE IN HIS TEACHER'S HOUSE. Written on a second-grade reading and interest level.

The Cam Jansen Series: Between the YOUNG CAM JANSEN and CAM JANSEN titles for beginning and advancing readers in grades 1 and 2–3 respectively, there are over 30 books, written by veteran author David A. Adler and published by Viking, about the resourceful, inquisitive gal with the photographic memory. Simple black-and-white line drawings by Susanna Natti accompany the text. (See the read-aloud plan for TODAY WAS A TERRIBLE DAY, written by Patricia Reilly Giff and illustrated by Susanna Natti.)

Clue Jr. Series: Each of these books, created by Parker C. Hinter and based on the board game by Parker Brothers, offers simple cases for readers to solve. The clues are found in the stories as well as the illustrations. Solutions follow each short case. Published by Scholastic; copyright Waddingtons Games Ltd. A great group read, car game, or holiday pastime for beginning-to-mid second-grade readers.

Judy Moody Series: Written by Megan McDonald and illustrated by Peter Reynolds (Candlewick). Here's a character sure to be remembered and certain to be loved by many. Enjoy free-spirited Judy's escapades with little bro "Stink," best friend Rocky, and "pest" friend Frank. Get the picture? Titles include JUDY MOODY, JUDY MOODY PREDICTS THE FUTURE, JUDY MOODY SAVES THE WORLD!, and JUDY MOODY GETS FAMOUS!

Amber Brown Series: Written by the zany and much-loved author Paula Danziger and illustrated by Tony Ross (cover art of some titles is done by Jacqueline Rogers), these books are published in hardcover by Putnam and in paperback by Apple Books/Scholastic. The main character is a contemporary third-grade gal with realistic problems and believable friends. She is funny, feisty, and vastly popular among independent readers on the advanced second- and beginning third-grade level. Titles include AMBER BROWN IS NOT A CRAYON, AMBER BROWN WANTS EXTRA CREDIT, FOREVER AMBER BROWN, GET READY FOR SECOND GRADE, AMBER BROWN, and IT'S A FAIR DAY, AMBER BROWN.

Riverside Kids Series: Written by the prolific Johanna Hurwitz, these numerous books feature Nora, Teddy, Elisa, and Russell. Suitable both for reading aloud and independent readers on a mid-second-grade level. Titles include BUSYBODY NORA, E IS FOR ELISA, RIP-ROARING RUSSELL, and SUPERDUPER TEDDY, and RUSSELL SPROUTS. Published by HarperCollins.

Third-Grade Detectives Series (Ready-for-Chapters): "Limited Edition" titles in this series include a teacher's guide. Interactive in style, these stories encourage the reader to help solve the cases that Mr. Merlin, beloved teacher and former spy, presents to his students. The first title, THE CLUE OF THE LEFT-HANDED ENVELOPE, involves secret codes and encourages working together to solve a problem. Written by George E. Stanley and illustrated by Salvatore Murdocca (Aladdin).

The Matt Christopher Series: The "#1 Sports series for kids" boasts the publisher, Little, Brown. Numerous titles by the late Christopher; recent titles are ghost-written. Titles include FAIRWAY PROBLEM, MASTER OF DISASTER, DIVE RIGHT IN, AT THE PLATE WITH ICHIRO, and ON THE BIKE WITH LANCE ARMSTRONG (sports biographies).

JUDY MOODY Text © 2000 by Megan McDonald.
Illustrations © 2000 by Peter Reynolds. Reproduced by permission
of the publisher Candlewick Press, Inc., Cambridge, MA.

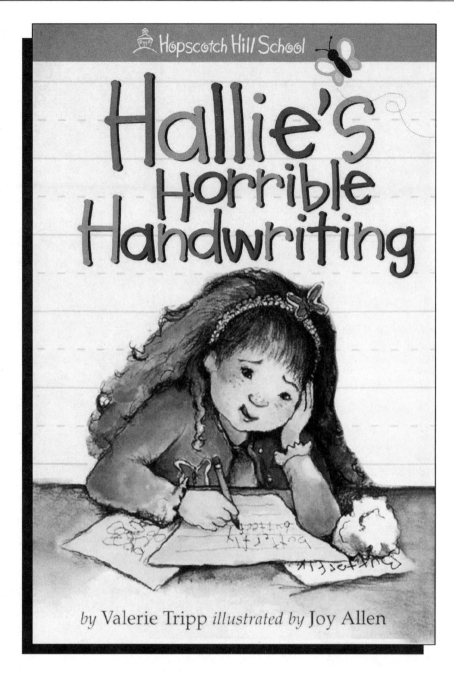

Cover of HALLIE'S HORRIBLE HANDWRITING copyright © 2003 by Pleasant Company, reprinted with permission.

Cover of THE HIGH-RISE PRIVATE EYES #1: THE CASE OF THE MISSING MONKEY written by Cynthia Rylant and illustrated by G. Brian Karas; copyright © 2000 by G. Brian Karas. Used by permission of HarperCollins Publishers.

Single Titles

WHY CAN'T I FLY?: A monkey named Minnie wants to learn to fly. She tries and she tries. "I can fly, I can fly, I can . . . flop," she says over and over until her friends come to her aid. Written by Rita Golden Gelman and illustrated by Jack Kent. Published by Scholastic.

ANNIE AND BO AND THE BIG SURPRISE: Written by Elizabeth Partridge and illustrated by Martha Weston, this "Dutton Easy Reader" is a sweet, wintry tale of two friends who manage to find the best surprises to give to each other; nine simple chapters.

SLEEPING UGLY: Written by Jane Yolen and illustrated by Diane Stanley, there is little doubt why this book published by Putnam goes far beyond the typical beginning reader in depth and craft. Princess Miserella is beautiful and mean, while Plain Jane is kind but has "a face to match her name." Humorous delivery of wishes and a healthy dose of misunderstanding will make this book a favorite among first- and second-grade readers.

THE BLUE RIBBON PUPPIES: This classic by Crockett Johnson, author of HAROLD AND THE PURPLE CRAYON, was first published by HarperCollins in 1958. It is the story of how a boy and a girl decide who should get the blue ribbons among the seven of the most adorable pups to be found in children's books.

THE CARROT SEED: Written by Ruth Krauss and illustrated by Crockett Johnson with sunny yellow pages, this is a perfect springtime book for beginning readers. First published by HarperCollins in 1945.

KEEP THE LIGHTS BURNING, ABBIE: Written by Peter Roop and Connie Roop and illustrated by Peter E. Hanson (Carolrhoda Books), this story is based on the account of a brave girl who kept a lighthouse lit during a storm off the coast of Maine in 1856. A note from the authors prefaces this tale with more details about the girl, who grew up to care for lighthouses her entire life.

ARTHUR'S HONEY BEAR: This Arthur is the classic creation of author/illustrator Lillian Hoban. Here Arthur is planning a Tag Sale. He is cleaning out his toy chest and must decide if he is too old for his honey bear. Will he sell him? Published by HarperCollins.

DANNY AND THE DINOSAUR: A classic by Syd Hoff about the adventures of Danny and his "dandy friend," published by HarperCollins. How can you argue with a dinosaur book for beginning readers?

THE HORSE IN HARRY'S ROOM: Another classic by Syd Hoff that is now a part of the I Can Read series published by HarperCollins, this is the story of Harry and his imaginary horse that cares not to roam but instead is content to stay in Harry's room.

PEARL AND WAGNER TWO GOOD FRIENDS: This "Dial Easy-To-Read," Level 2 title is written by former teacher and author of over 75 books for children, Kate McMullen. A three-chapter book delightfully illustrated by R. W. Alley, who aptly depicts the companionship and comical repartee that transpire between this rabbit and mouse, two good friends and two great characters.

HARRY'S DOG: Written by Barbara Ann Porte and illustrated by Yossi Abolafia, this Greenwillow title is as warm and wonderful as the dog that causes Dad to sneeze and Harry to come up with a plan. A favorite early reader.

THE LITTLE FISH THAT GOT AWAY: This book, first published in 1956 by David McKay Company, is written by Bernadine Cook and features Crockett Johnson's distinctive art, which beckons the new reader and promises a delightful reading adventure. It delivers in this chronicle of a boy's experience with fishing. Giggles guaranteed.

SEBASTIAN (SUPER SLEUTH) AND THE CRUMMY YUMMIES CAPER: "A Dog-gone Growling Good Mystery!" written by Mary Blount Christian and illustrated by Lisa McCue and starring a memorable sheep dog that makes one heckuva hound dog. Published by Bantam.

TALES FOR THE PERFECT CHILD: A Dell reader dedicated to "perfect children everywhere," filled with seven stories about decidedly not-so-perfect children. Sure to tickle the tummy. Written by Florence Parry Heide and illustrated by Victoria Chess.

MATTHEW JACKSON MEETS THE WALL: One of Polk Street School's most beloved kids moves away from New York and the Polk Street School to a new neighborhood full of challenges. For more accomplished readers. Written by Patricia Reilly Giff and illustrated by Blanche Sims (Dell).

GOONEY BIRD GREENE: Written by Newbery winner Lois Lowry and illustrated by Middy Thomas (Houghton Mifflin). A most unusual free spirit joins a memorably typical second-grade class, and nobody is the same from the moment she sets foot in the door. For more accomplished readers.

THE HERO OF THIRD GRADE: A new town, newly divorced parents, a new school in April: Is Randall's life ruined, or will he become a hero on the order of the Scarlet Pimpernel? Written by Alice DeLaCroix and illustrated by Cynthia Fisher (Holiday House). For more accomplished readers.

ANNA, GRANPA, AND THE BIG STORM: The story of a girl and her grandfather, who get caught in the legendary Great Blizzard of 1888 en route to a spelling bee. Written by Carla Stevens and illustrated by Margot Thomas (Clarion).

Begin with the First, Then Pass It On . . .

Listed below are selected, well-loved, well-known classic chapter book series that lend themselves well to the read-aloud experience and are sure to enrapture first and second graders. Begin with one and then send a list of titles home (see Parent Pull-Out Pages) so parents can continue the adventures, or let more able readers loose to carry on with the characters on their own as their reading skills develop. What better incentive to take it up a notch!

The Littles: A treasury of tales written by John Peterson and illustrated by Roberta Carter Clark (Scholastic); about a family six inches tall with tails. Titles include

    THE LITTLES

    THE LITTLES AND THE BIG STORM

    THE LITTLES AND THE TRASH TINIES

    THE LITTLES TO THE RESCUE

    THE LITTLES GO TO SCHOOL

    THE LITTLES GIVE A PARTY

    THE LITTLES AND THE LOST CHILDREN

    TOM LITTLE'S GREAT HALLOWEEN SCARE

Mrs. Piggle-Wiggle: A character children will love who endears herself to the kids in her neighborhood because she smells like cookies, she lives in an up-side-down house, and she was once married to a pirate! But best of all, she helps children overcome any problem, from hating baths to eating too slowly. Pure delight, fine fun; these books are written by Betty MacDonald and illustrated by Hilary Knight (with the exception of FARM, which was illustrated by Maurice Sendak); published by HarperCollins. Titles include

MRS. PIGGLE-WIGGLE

MRS. PIGGLE-WIGGLE'S MAGIC

MRS. PIGGLE WIGGLE'S FARM

HELLO, MRS. PIGGLE-WIGGLE

The Hilarious Adventures of Paddington: Who doesn't recognize the adorable bear with the yellow hat and blue overcoat with a tag attached that says, "Please look after this BEAR thank you"? Sweet, humorous, gentle tales sure to please five- to seven-year-olds, are written by Michael Bond with illustrations by Peggy Fortnum (Dell). Titles include

A BEAR CALLED PADDINGTON

MORE ABOUT PADDINGTON

PADDINGTON HELPS OUT

PADDINGTON AT LARGE

PADDINGTON AT WORK

PADDINGTON ABROAD

PADDINGTON MARCHES ON

My Father's Dragon: Three tales written by Ruth Stiles Gannett and illustrated in black-and-white by Ruth Chrisman Gannett (Random House), the first of which is a Newbery Honor Award winner. The first of these books of pure silliness paired with adventure is about a boy's trip to Wild Island to save a dragon. This set of books has been winning the hearts and imaginations of children since it was published in 1948. In addition to MY FATHER'S DRAGON, the trilogy includes

ELMER AND THE DRAGON, and

THE DRAGONS OF BLUELAND

The Spiderwick Chronicles: A new series that will be five books in all, by an award-winning team that has garnered much interest as a solid choice for fantasy lovers who can't quite tackle (or lift) the Harry Potter series; by Tony DiTerlizzi and Holly Black (Simon & Schuster). Titles include

THE FIELD GUIDE

THE SEEING STONE

LUCINDA'S SECRET

See Parent Pull-Out Pages for a handy sheet listing these books that you can send home to parents.

Text and illustrations copyright © 2003 THE SPIDERWICK CHRONICLES: THE FIELD GUIDE written by Tony DiTerlizzi and illustrated by Holly Black. Used with permission of Simon & Schuster Books for Young Readers, a division of Simon & Schuster Children's Publishing.

Text and illustrations copyright © 2003 THE SPIDERWICK CHRONICLES: THE SEEING STONE written by Tony DiTerlizzi and illustrated by Holly Black. Used with permission of Simon & Schuster Books for Young Readers, a division of Simon & Schuster Children's Publishing.

Text and illustrations copyright © 2003 THE SPIDERWICK CHRONICLES: LUCINDA'S SECRET written by Tony DiTerlizzi and illustrated by Holly Black. Used with permission of Simon & Schuster Books for Young Readers, a division of Simon & Schuster Children's Publishing.

Snap Crackle Poppity-Pop: Overcoming Poetry's Bad Rap

You've heard how "it's not your father's Chevrolet." Well, trust me, says this saleswoman of verse, today's poetry is not what you remember from when you were forced to memorize and regurgitate eight lines in eighth grade. Today's poetry comes in all flavors and styles, and just like cars, there's sure to be one in the lot to please you. Trust me.

Read through recently published volumes of poetry and you'll be amazed at the kid appeal. Peruse, choose, and flag your favorites, then use them to augment a read-aloud or round out a unit of study. Want a laugh? Need to make a point? Wish to commemorate a special day, celebrate a holiday, or pay tribute to an important figure in history? Poetry, please.

But go beyond that. Build a poetry pause into every school day. Before lunch, before recess, after a tough round of math or a grueling spelling quiz, lighten the load. Poetry, please.

You'll find the poems in the books listed below cover a myriad of topics, from inventions to dirty laundry. Some are collections on a specific topic written by a number of authors, while others are collections on varied subjects written by a single author. Get out your sticky-notes and label selections by theme. Think of it as your poetry cookbook. Catalog your favorites, whatever the reason. Who needs a reason? Keep books of verse handy. There's nothing like rhythm and rhyme, short and sweet, to capture and enrapture today's children. Trust me.

- THE REASON FOR THE PELICAN, written by John Ciardi and illustrated by Dominic Catalano (Boyds Mills Press); "35th Anniversary Edition" of this first book of poetry by a Hall-of-Famer among the best and finest poets for children.

- YOU KNOW WHO, written by John Ciardi and illustrated by Edward Gorey (Boyds Mills Press); poems about and for the less-than-perfect peanut.

- YOU READ TO ME, I'LL READ TO YOU, written by John Ciardi and illustrated by Edward Gorey (HarperCollins). You read the poems in black and children in first grade and up are encouraged to read the poems in blue.

- FIREFLIES AT MIDNIGHT, written by Marilyn Singer and illustrated by Ken Robbins (Atheneum); profiles of everyday, summery creatures told from their point of view include the otter, monarch, bat, red fox, horse, and spider. Delightful word play. Recite on days when you read aloud books about the animal, such as STELLALUNA, for which a read-aloud plan can be found in the first part of this resource. Or use them as part of a more in-depth unit of study.

Cover art, text, and illustrations copyright © 2003 FIREFLIES AT MIDNIGHT written by Marilyn Singer and illustrated by Ken Robbins. Used with permission of Atheneum Books for Young Readers, a division of Simon & Schuster Children's Publishing.

- DEAR WORLD, by Takayo Noda (Dial). Pause to celebrate details of our every-day world, from "dear snow" to "dear car," with these spare poems accompanied by bright, engaging, cut-paper collages. Perfect pauses.

- AMBER WAS BRAVE, ESSIE WAS SMART: THE STORY OF AMBER AND ESSIE TOLD HERE IN POEMS AND PICTURES, by Vera B. Williams (Greenwillow); a story of two sisters facing life's ups and downs together. The sadly realistic, touching, funny, sobering, award-winning tale of two sisters told in free verse.

- DIRTY LAUNDRY PILE: POEMS IN DIFFERENT VOICES, selected by Paul B. Janeczko and illustrated by Melissa Sweet (Greenwillow). Animals and inani-mate objects tell it like it is from their perspective, everything from a vacuum cleaner to a mosquito—and of course, the dirty laundry pile.

- I INVITED A DRAGON TO DINNER AND OTHER POEMS TO MAKE YOU LAUGH OUT LOUD, illustrated by Chris L. Demarest (Philomel). Don't miss "Coming Unscrewed" by Claudia Harrington, about a lady who took off her head because she didn't fit in her bed, or "The Attic" by Dave Crawley, in which a rum-ble, grumble upstairs leads to fear of the babble in the depths of the basement below, in this hilarious collection by a variety of authors. Time out!

- THE FROGS WORE RED SUSPENDERS, rhymes by Jack Prelutsky and illus-trated by Petra Mathers (Greenwillow); zippy, zany poems and pictures about people and animals in places and spaces from here to there all over the world: from Minneapolis to Indianapolis, from the store to the pudding vat. Now how can you not laugh at that?

- A CHILD'S CALENDAR, written by John Updike and illustrated by Trina Schart Hyman (Holiday House). This lovely edition won a Caldecott Honor Medal.

- PIECES A YEAR IN POEMS & QUILTS, by Anna Grossnickle Hines (HarperCollins); illustrated with quilts; includes afterword on the story behind the quilts.

- WINTER POEMS, selected by Barbara Rogasky and illustrated by Trina Schart Hyman (Scholastic). Twenty-five poems from Shakespeare to Sandburg to Japa-nese haiku celebrate the season.

- IT'S VALENTINE'S DAY, poems by Jack Prelutsky and illustrated by Yossi Abolafia (HarperCollins); a non-fattening treat for this holiday.

- MY BOOK OF FUNNY VALENTINES, written by Margo Lundell and illustrated by Nate Evans (Scholastic); silly fun.

- EASTER BUDS ARE SPRINGING: POEMS FOR EASTER, selected by Lee Bennett Hopkins and illustrated by Tomie de Paola (Boyds Mills Press).

- SUMMERSAULTS, by Douglas Florian (Greenwillow); all about wonderful, deli-cious, delightful summer. Companion to WINTER EYES. Sure to be a favorite: "Three Words" (Clue: back to school).

- ANNA'S GARDEN SONGS, poems by Mary Q. Steele and illustrated by Lena Anderson (HarperCollins).

- ANNA'S SUMMER SONGS, poems by Mary Q. Steele and illustrated by Lena Anderson (HarperCollins).

- IT'S HALLOWEEN, poems by Jack Prelutsky and illustrated by Marylin Hafner (HarperCollins); pure Prelutsky humor.

- HIST WHIST, written by e.e. cummings and illustrated by Deborah Kogan Ray (Crown); illustrated poem.

- LITTLE TREE, written by e.e. cummings and illustrated by Deborah Kogan Ray (Crown); a Christmas poem illustrated with dreamy paintings.

- IT'S CHRISTMAS, poems by Jack Prelutsky and illustrated by Marylin Hafner (Greenwillow); silly fun, re-readable.

- THE NIGHT BEFORE CHRISTMAS, written by Clement Moore and illustrated by Tomie dePaola (Holiday House).

- FATHERS, MOTHERS, SISTERS, BROTHERS: A COLLECTION OF FAMILY POEMS, written by Mary Ann Hoberman and illustrated by Marylin Hafner (Penguin).

- SING A SONG OF POPCORN: EVERY CHILD'S BOOK OF POEMS, selected by Beatrice Schenk de Regniers, Eva Moore, Mary Michaels White, Jane Carr and illustrated by nine Caldecott Medal artists (Scholastic); in memory of Arnold Lobel.

- ANIMALS ANIMALS, selected and illustrated by Eric Carle (Philomel); a thick volume of poems about animals from the ant to the yak, richly illustrated by the master of collage.

- SCRANIMALS, poems by Jack Prelutsky and illustrated by Peter Sis (Greenwillow). This duo collaborates with successful results. These poems focus on scrambled animals and veggies: perfect fare for this age group. Sample "sweet porcupineapple/unflappable chap" and the "detested radishark" and more beastly creatures on Scranimal Island.

- BLUEBERRY INK, written by Eve Merriam and illustrated by Hans Wilhelm (HarperCollins); a lively collection from "I'm sweet says the beet" to "Is it robin o'clock?/Is it five after wing?"

- WHERE THE SIDEWALK ENDS, by Shel Silverstein (HarperCollins); zany, zippy, crazy fun, but thoughtful, too. A must-have collection.

- A LIGHT IN THE ATTIC, by Shel Silverstein (HarperCollins); more by the prince of poetry for children.

- NOT A COPPER PENNY IN ME HOUSE: POEMS FROM THE CARIBBEAN, written by Monica Gunning and illustrated by Frane Lessac (Boyds Mills Press); lyrical portrayal of a girl's life.

- TYRANNOSAURUS WAS A BEAST, written by Jack Prelutsky and illustrated by Arnold Lobel (Greenwillow); relates facts about the favorites in light verse.

- THE ICE CREAM STORE, written by Dennis Lee and illustrated by David McPhail (HarperCollins). Take a trip with the kids in this collection of poems that "are like an Ice cream store/'Cause there's chocolate, and vanilla,/And there's maple and there's more."

- GOOD BOOKS, GOOD TIMES!, selected by Lee Bennett Hopkins and illustrated by Harvey Stevenson (HarperCollins); poems that celebrate books.

- IF I WERE IN CHARGE OF THE WORLD AND OTHER WORRIES, written by Judith Viorst and illustrated by Lynne Cherry (Aladdin); subjects of poems range from "Wishes and Worries" to "Facts of Life" to "Thanks and No Thanks." One of my favorites is the one in which Cinderella takes a closer look at the prince and decides, "I think I'll just pretend that this glass slipper feels too tight."

- LOCUST POCUS! A BOOK TO BUG YOU, written by Douglas Kaine McKelvey and illustrated by Richard Egielski (Philomel); poems not for the squeamish.

- HERE'S WHAT YOU CAN DO WHEN YOU CAN'T FIND YOUR SHOE, written by Andrea Perry and illustrated by Alan Snow (Atheneum); see the read-aloud plan.

On the subject of teaching and sharing poetry with children, see

- PASS THE POETRY, PLEASE!; 3d ed., by Lee Bennett Hopkins (HarperCollins)

Book-Related Resources
for Busy Teachers

RESOURCE BOOKS

These handy guides ought to be on the shelves of every school and public library. If you can manage to add them to your classroom resource shelf, all the better. They are accessible, informative, and user-friendly.

- **The New Read-aloud Handbook, 5th ed.**, by Jim Trelease (Penguin Books)

- **Hey! Listen to This: Stories to Read-Aloud**, by Jim Trelease (Penguin Books)

- **Reading Magic: Why Reading Aloud to Our Children Will Change Their Lives Forever**, by Mem Fox (Harcourt)

- **Let's Read About . . . Finding Books They'll Love to Read**, by Bernice Cullinan (Scholastic)

- **Michele Landsberg's Guide to Children's Books**, by Michele Landsberg (Penguin Books)

- **Pass the Poetry, Please!; 3d ed.**, by Lee Bennett Hopkins (HarperCollins)

The following texts devoted to reading instruction contain informative sections on reading aloud to children:

- **The Art of Teaching Reading**, by Lucy McCormick Calkins (Longman)

- **Access for All: Closing the Gap for Children in Early Education**, by Susan B. Neuman, Donna C. Celano, Albert N. Greco, and Pamela Shue (International Reading Association)

- **Children Achieving: Best Practices in Early Literacy**, edited by Susan B. Neuman and Kathleen Roskos (International Reading Association)

- **Read-Alouds with Young Children**, by Robin Campbell (International Reading Association)

- **Guided Reading: Good First Teaching for All Children**, by Irene C. Fountas and Guy Su Pinnell (Heinemann)

- **Word Matters: Teaching Phonics and Spelling in the Reading and Writing Classroom**, by Guy Su Pinnell and Irene C. Fountas (Heinemann)

PERIODICALS

The advantage of periodicals is that they provide up-to-the-minute information about the latest, most recent additions and editions, and timely articles of interest related to children's literature.

The Horn Book Magazine: Published every other month, this magazine, founded in 1924, is chock full of reviews, publisher ads, editorials, and features reflecting a deep passion for and commitment to enduring quality in books for children and young adults. Address: 56 Roland St., Suite 200, Boston, MA 02129; Telephone: 800-325-1170; Fax: 617-628-0882; Internet: magazine@hbook.com. Subscription: $45, individual; $55, institutional. Special introductory rates.

Booklist: Published twice monthly September through June and monthly in July and August by the American Library Association, this is a highly regarded source of reviews on all literature pertaining to children. Address: Kable Fulfillment Services, Agency Processing Team, 308 E. Hitt St., Mount Morris, IL 61054; Telephone: 888-350-0949; Fax: 815-734-1252; e-mail: blnk@kable.com. US subscriptions: $79.95.

Book Links: Published six times per year by the American Library Association, this resource connects children's books, K–8, to curricula in science, social studies, and language arts. Included in each issue are suggestions for novels to teach, advice, author interviews, reviews, and thematic bibliographies. Address: PO Box 615, Mt. Morris, IL 61054-7566; Telephone: 888-350-0950; Fax: 815-734-1252; e-mail: blnk@kable.com. Subscription: $27.95.

School Library Journal: Founded in 1954, and now in both print and online formats, this resource serves librarians in school and public libraries. It boasts more book reviews than any other resource of its kind. Address: PO Box 16178, North Hollywood, CA 91615-6178; Telephone: 800-595-1066; Fax: 818-487-4566; e-mail: slj@reedbusiness.com. Subscription: $124.

The Reading Teacher: Published eight times a year for members of the International Reading Association, this magazine targets elementary school teachers. Address: 800 Barksdale Rd., PO Box 8139, Newark, DE 19714-8139; Telephone: 800-336-7323; e-mail: www.reading.org.

Kirkus Review: Founded in 1933, this resource is currently available in print and online editions. Specialists in the field review 5,000 titles per year, of which children's books is one category. Telephone: 646-654-5865; Fax: 646-654-5518; e-mail: mhazzard@vnubuspubs.com. Contact for rates and packages.

Also:

The **Children's Book Council**: This nonprofit organization is the official sponsor of National Children's Book Week and Young People's Poetry Week. It is "dedicated to encouraging literacy and the use and enjoyment of children's books." The CBC distributes a variety of useful materials about books and reading. Their catalog contains posters, friezes, streamers, bookmarks, postcards, and a variety of other products for sale. Address: 568 Broadway, New York, NY 10012; Telephone: 212-966-1990; Fax: 212-966-2073. Credit card orders for materials: 800-999-2160 or e-mail: catalogs@cbcbooks.org. (See Web site listing below.)

WEB SITES

Want to learn more about children's literature from the computer screen? Here is a list of professional Web sites that deliver a wealth of information on books for children. A list of publisher Web sites follows.

- **www.trelease-on-reading.com**—Web site of Jim Trelease, author of *The Read-Aloud Handbook* (Penguin Books)

- **www.ala.org**—American Library Association Web site; link example: www.ala.org/booklist/—Lists notable children's titles published in the past year arranged by age.

- **www.alastore.ala.org**—The graphics catalog published by the American Library Association (ALA); features a variety of items including the popular READ celebrity posters, T-shirts, lanyards, decals, pencils, bookmarks, and more.

- **www.slj.com/articles/articles/articlesindex.asp**—*School Library Journal* link; see "Best Books of the Year."

- **www.readingrainbow.org**—Reading Rainbow site; includes a listing of all the books covered on its episodes since the program's inception.

- **www.cbcbooks.org**—Web site of Children's Book Council, a nonprofit trade association of children's book publishers, the purpose of which is to promote reading in children. For information, tips, and activities for Children's Book Week, celebrated annually in November, go to http://cbcbooks.org/html/book_week.html.

- **www.acs.ucalgary.ca/~dkbrown/**—Visit this site for an in-depth look at various aspects of children's books; developed by David K. Brown, director of Doucette Library of Teaching Resources at the University of Calgary, Alberta, Canada.

- **www.reading.org and www.readingonline.org**—International Reading Association Web site. Go to www.reading.org/choics for downloadable Children's Choices lists, those books deemed favorites by children themselves; there is also a Teachers' Choices list of those books chosen by teachers that coordinate well with curriculum.

- **www.earlyreading.info**—This Web site, developed by the Regional Educational Laboratory at Pacific Resources for Education and Learning (PREL), helps teachers and others who work with children in pre-K–3 meet the challenge set by the Reading First initiative of having all students in the United States read at grade level by the time they reach third grade.

- **www.readwritethink.org**–focuses on reading and language arts; provided by the International Reading Association (IRA) and the National Council of Teachers of English (NCTE).

- **www.rifreadingplanet.org**—an interactive site for parents and children.

- **http://marcopolo.worldcom.com**—goal is to provide "the highest quality standards-based Internet content and professional development to K–12 teachers and students" in the United States and beyond.

- **www.edu.gov.on.ca/eng/document/reports/reading/reading.pdf**—early reading strategies.

- **sago.tamu.edu/aapr/WhtHseReport.pdf**—the White House Summit on Early Childhood Cognitive Development; includes "The Role of Parents and Grandparents in Children's Cognitive Development: Focus on Language and Literacy" by Dorothy Strickland.

- **http://www.mcps.k12.md.us/curriculum/english/earlylit_cont.htm**—timeline of expected reading skills from kindergarten to grade 2 from Montgomery County Public Schools in Rockville, Maryland.

- **www.ncrel.org/sdrs/areas/issues/content/cntareas/reading/li100.htm**— "Critical Issues Addressing the Literacy Needs of Emergent and Early Readers"; North Central Educational Laboratory.

- **www.icdlbooks.org**—International Children's Digital Library Web site.

- **www.readingrockets.org**—national service of public television station WETA in Washington, D.C.; offers "information about teaching kids to read and helping those who struggle."

Online Bookstores:

- **www.amazon.com**—the largest online bookstore

- **www.bn.com**—Barnes & Noble online

Publishers

To order directly from publishers, visit their Web sites for ordering information. You will note that for the larger publishers, such as Simon & Schuster, the imprints have links from the main Web address. In some publishing companies, imprints act independently of one another; in other publishing houses, they share departments.

- **Boyds Mills Press:** www.boydsmillspress.com

Imprint: Wordsong (poetry)

- **Candlewick Press:** www.candlewick.com

- **Clarion:** www.houghtonmifflinbooks.com

- **Farrar, Straus & Giroux**: www.fsgbooks.com

- **Harcourt Children's Book Division**: www.harcourtbooks.com

Imprints: Gulliver Books, Silverwhistle

- **HarperCollins Children's Books:** www.harperchildrens.com

Imprints: HarperFestival; Joanna Cotler Books, Greenwillow

- **Henry Holt**: www.henryholt.com

- **Holiday House:** www.holidayhouse.com

- **Houghton Mifflin**: www.houghtonmifflinbooks.com

- **Hyperion Books for Children:** www.hyperionchildrensbooks.com

An imprint of Disney Children's Book Group

- **Lee & Low**: www.leeandlow.com

- **Little, Brown**: www.littlebrown.com

- **Penguin Group USA**: www.us.penguingroup.com

Imprints: Dial Books for Young Readers, Dutton Children's Books, G.P. Putnam's Sons, Philomel, Putnam, Puffin, Penguin, Viking, Grosset & Dunlap

- **Random House**: www.randomhouse.com/kids/

Imprints: Knopf Delacorte Dell Young Readers Group, Random House Children's Books, Golden Books for Young Readers, Crown

- **Scholastic**: www.scholastic.com

Imprints: Scholastic Press, Cartwheel Books, Blue Sky Press, Orchard Books

- **Simon & Schuster Children's Publishing Division**: www.simonsayskids.com

Imprints: Aladdin, Atheneum, Margaret K. McElderry Books, Simon & Schuster Books for Young Readers, Paula Wiseman Books

- **Albert Whitman & Company**: www.albertwhitman.com

And the Winner Is...

AWARDS THAT CELEBRATE CHILDREN'S BOOKS

Numerous awards honor children's books, and if you know about them, you'll have a source for the best of the best in the field of children's literature. A handy reference is *The Horn Book* (www.hbook.com), which announces recent award winners in the back of each issue in a section entitled, "The Hunt Breakfast." Another useful Web site for a listing of children's book awards is www.childrenslit.com.

For picture books, look for news of the **Caldecott Award** winners in the spring of each year. (See Parent Pull-Out Pages for more on this prestigious award and a partial list of winners.) This award is presented annually by the American Library Association, and listings can be found on its Web site, www.ala.org.

Many states also give awards, such as the **Texas Bluebonnet Award** (www.txla.org/groups/tba), Minnesota's **Maud Hart Lovelace Book Award** (www. isd77.k12.mn.us/lovelace/lovelace.html), New York's **Charlotte Award** (www.nysreading.org/awards), and Wyoming's **Indian Paintbrush Book Award** (www.ccpls.org/html/indianp.html). Go to www.carr.lib.md.us/read/stateawardsbks.htm for a general listing of state awards and their Web sites.

An international award worth noting is the **Hans Christian Andersen Award** (www.ibby.org/seiten/04_andersen.htm), considered to be the most prestigious award in children's literature in the world. Bestowed every two years by the International Board on Books for Young People (IBBY), it honors an author whose work has made a significant contribution internationally to children's literature.

Three English awards are the **Carnegie Medal**, which recognizes an outstanding children's book written in English and first published in the United Kingdom; the **Kate Greenaway Medal**, which parallels the Caldecott Award (www.carnegiegreenaway.org.uk); and the **Smarties Book Prize,** which is awarded annually to the best children's book published in the United Kingdom (www.booktrusted.com/nestle).

In Canada, the **Canadian Library Association Book of the Year for Children Award** (www.cla.ca/awards/boyc.htm) honors a book of literary distinction, while the **Amelia Frances Howard-Gibbon Medal (**www.cla.ca/awards/afhg.htm) is awarded to an outstanding illustrated book written by a Canadian and published in Canada .

Following is a selected list of notable awards presented in the United States of particular interest to teachers of first and second grades.

IRA Children's Choice Award: Each year 10,000 students from across the country are asked to choose their favorite books from a list of recently published titles. Votes are tabulated and books are grouped according to reading levels. The lists are generated and distributed by the International Reading Association (IRA) in conjunction with the Children's Book Council. They appear in the October issue of the IRA journal, *The Reading Teacher.* (**Teachers' Choice Awards,** a list of 30 books rated by teams of teachers, librarians, and reading specialists, are announced in the November issue of *Reading Teacher.*) Copies can be obtained for $1 accompanied by a self-addressed, 9-inch-by-12-inch envelope, from IRA, 800 Barksdale Rd., PO Box 8139, Newark, DE 19714-8139, or lists can be downloaded as PDF files from the IRA Web site: www.reading.org.

The Golden Kite Award: This annual award, established in 1973, is announced in late spring. It is presented to a member of the Society of Children's Book Writers and Illustrators for excellence in the field of children's books. Statuettes are awarded in four categories: fiction, nonfiction, picture book text, and picture illustration. Web site: www.scbwi.org.

The Charlotte Zolotow Award: Named for the well-known picture book author and awarded annually for outstanding text in a picture book. Go to www.so emadison.wisc.edu/ccbc/zolotow.htm for more information.

Boston Globe-Horn Book Award: Awarded annually in the fall for excellence in literature for children and young adults in the categories of fiction or poetry, nonfiction, and illustration. Winners are listed in *The Horn Book* in January. Web site: www.hbook.com.

American Booksellers BookSense Book of the Year Award: The ABBY award was renamed this in 2000. It is presented each year to the children's book voted by members as the title they most enjoy recommending to customers. Web site: www.bookweb.org/news/awards/

Laura Ingalls Wilder Award: Presented every two years by the Association for Library Services to Children (ALSC) to an author or illustrator whose books, published in the United States, have made a lasting contribution to the field of children's books over a period of years. Go to www.ala.org for more information.

Robert F. Sibert Award Informational Book Award: Awarded annually to the author of the best informational book for children. Go to www.ala.org for more information.

Coretta Scott King Awards: In honor of Martin Luther King Jr., awards are given annually to an African-American author and an African-American illustrator whose books provide inspiration and educate. Honors are also awarded. Go to www.ala.org for more information.

Jane Addams Book Award: Awarded to the author of a book that promotes peace, social justice, and equality of the sexes and races. Go to www.janeaddamspeace. org for more information.

Scott O'Dell Award for Historical Fiction: Awarded for a book for children or young adults published in English in the United States and set in the Americas. Web site: www.scottodell.com.

Lee Bennett Hopkins Poetry Award: Founded by Hopkins in 1993 to promote poetry, this award is presented annually to an American poet or anthologist for the most outstanding new book of children's poetry published in the previous calendar year. Web site: www.pabook.libraries.psu.edu/hopkinsaward.html.

Parent Pull-Out Pages

Raising Readers

Tips and Techniques for Parents

by Judy Bradbury

HOW TO KEEP YOUR YOUNG READER READING

Your child is reading on his own! You have a right to be proud and amazed at how your son or daughter went from gnawing on chunky board books while nestled on your lap to reading sentences in paragraphs and pausing at periods in just a few short years.

Go ahead. Be proud. Listen as your child reads to you. Praise often, and supply your child with lots and lots of books and magazines.

But don't push that kid off your lap yet.

Parents often think that as children get older they outgrow read-alouds. Not so! Continue reading aloud to your child everyday. Shift to picture storybooks, which have abundant illustrations but feature more text than simpler picture books. Sample short chapter books, which are usually 60–80 pages in length, with chapters three to five pages long. Gradually introduce longer books (if appropriate in content) when your child can sit and listen for 15 minutes or more.

Didn't read aloud when your child was younger? It's never too late to start. In *Becoming a Nation of Readers,* experts in the field of reading advocate reading aloud to children throughout their school years—right up to graduation! Begin with short read-aloud sessions. But begin them, nevertheless, and don't give up. As you continue the routine of nightly read-alouds, not only will you become a more relaxed reader, but your child's attention span and interest will increase as well. Choose books together and vary the menu. Try fantasy, nonfiction, poetry, and mysteries. In additon to the Children's Book Corner series, an excellent resource is *The Read-Aloud Handbook* by Jim Trelease.

Research abounds citing the benefits of reading aloud to children. Not only does it foster a love of books, but parents also find children truly value this special time together. Reading aloud will improve your child's reading skills by developing listening habits, increasing attention span, enhancing concept development, and building listening, speaking, reading, and writing vocabularies. This translates into success in school and life.

But here's the biggest benefit: Reading aloud helps your child come to know that between the covers of books lies a limitless source of adventures restricted only by the hours one has to devote to that next good book.

And the next, natural step is choosing a good book to read to yourself.

Children's Book Corner: A READ-ALOUD Resource with Tips, Techniques, and Plans for Teachers, Librarians, and Parents, by Judy Bradbury. Westport, CT: Libraries Unlimited, 2004

Raising Readers

Tips and Techniques for Parents

by Judy Bradbury

READ-ALOUD TIPS AND TECHNIQUES

Parents eager to help their children achieve success in school often hear the advice, *Read aloud to your kids.* Okay, you say, I can do that. But are there tricks to reading aloud effectively?

Yes, but they are simple and easy to learn. Incorporate these basic strategies, and you'll soon find yourself looking forward to reading more of that book you've been sharing daily with your child. *What's going to happen next?* you wonder. A love of reading instilled in your child, that's what.

Techniques the Experts Use:

1. Read aloud stories that appeal to you. Everyday. Choose those that make you giggle, or sit on the edge of your seat. If a book makes you want to keep reading even when the soup is boiling over, it's a winner. If you love a book, you'll convey that to your child. If, on the other hand, you aren't enthused about the story, you'll probably give that away, too. Don't hesitate to reread favorites.

2. Skim the book or chapter before reading it aloud. Consider content and length with your child in mind. Become familiar with the plot so you can read with expression. When the character is frightened, shake! When the forest is creepy and spooky, whisper, and when something silly happens, enjoy those giggles right along with your child. Narrow your eyes, raise your eyebrows, lower your voice. Show fear, happiness, sadness, surprise. Draw your child into the story with the first sentence and make the last line memorable. Enjoy the illustrations. With chapter books, you'll find your child will beg you not to stop reading, and he'll reach for that book with anticipation tomorrow. Good, good, good. Because, remember, our mantra is *Read everyday*.

3. Choose a cozy, distraction-free spot to enjoy your read-aloud time. Wrap yourself and your child around the book. Cuddle up, cover up, lie head-to-head beneath the reading lamp. Do whatever will make your daily read-aloud time special, a time your child will cherish, savor, look forward to, and remember.

4. So, then, read aloud daily. And not just with your first or second grader, but with your middle-schooler, too. Reading aloud is the *single most important thing* you can do to improve your child's attitude toward reading. And reading aloud is one of the best gifts you can give to your child. It's free, it's easy, and it's rewarding for everyone involved. It expands your child's horizons and introduces one of life's most satisfying pleasures: the enjoyment that comes from the myriad wonders found between the covers of a book.

Children's Book Corner: A READ-ALOUD Resource with Tips, Techniques, and Plans for Teachers, Librarians, and Parents, by Judy Bradbury. Westport, CT: Libraries Unlimited, 2004

Raising Readers

Tips and Techniques for Parents

by Judy Bradbury

TOO OLD?

Once children can recognize their numbers and letters, there's no need or time for picture books.

Don't waste time reading picture books to first and second graders. Bring on those BIG KID books!

Older children don't want to read picture books. They're for babies.

If you've heard arguments like these and wondered if you're first or second grader is too old for picture books, relax. What better time is there than when your child is excited by her growing independence with print, to foster that enthusiasm with books that spark the senses?

Keep reading picture books with your child. Strive to find those that appeal to your child's interests. Look for picture storybooks that feature more complex stories than simple picture books. These are perfect for read-alouds with your budding reader. A few titles are listed below, but there are shelves full of these bountiful wonders that merge print and pictures to produce a memorable, engaging reading experience.

Too old? *Hogwash.*

Must-Not-Miss Picture Storybooks for Six- to Eight-Year-Olds

- IRA SLEEPS OVER, by Ira Waber (Houghton Mifflin)

- ALEXANDER AND THE TERRIBLE, HORRIBLE, NO GOOD, VERY BAD DAY, written by Judith Viorst and illustrated by Ray Cruz (Atheneum)

- GEORGE AND MARTHA, by James Marshall (Houghton Mifflin)

- STELLA LOUELLA'S RUNAWAY BOOK, by Lisa Campbell Ernst (Simon & Schuster)

- BARN DANCE!, written by Bill Martin Jr. and John Archambault and illustrated by Ted Rand (Holt)

- BIGFOOT CINDERRRRRELLA, written by Tony Johnston and illustrated by James Warhola (Putnam)

Children's Book Corner: A READ-ALOUD Resource with Tips, Techniques, and Plans for Teachers, Librarians, and Parents, by Judy Bradbury. Westport, CT: Libraries Unlimited, 2004

- KNOTS ON A COUNTING ROPE, written by Bill Martin Jr. and John Archambault and illustrated by Ted Rand (Holt)

- THE LITTLE OLD LADY WHO WAS NOT AFRAID OF ANYTHING, written by Linda Williams and illustrated by Megan Lloyd (HarperCollins)

- WHO'S AFRAID OF THE BIG BAD BOOK?, by Lauren Child (Hyperion)

- AXLE ANNIE, written by Robin Pulver and illustrated by Tedd Arnold (Puffin)

Must-Not-Miss Authors

- Tomie dePaola

- Bill Peet

- Jane Yolen

- Tedd Arnold

- Mark Teague

- John Ciardi

For a landmark book that explores the how, what, and why of hurrying our children to grow up, and the effect this has on them, see THE HURRIED CHILD: GROWING UP TOO FAST TOO SOON, 3d ed., written by David Elkind (Perseus Publishing).

Children's Book Corner: A READ-ALOUD Resource with Tips, Techniques, and Plans for Teachers, Librarians, and Parents, by Judy Bradbury. Westport, CT: Libraries Unlimited, 2004

Raising Readers

Tips and Techniques for Parents

by Judy Bradbury

RESOURCES FOR PARENTS

Want to learn more about the benefits of books? Check out these references.

Books

These are not research-dense, sleep-inducing texts; they're interesting reading!

- **The New Read-Aloud Handbook, 5th ed.,** by Jim Trelease (Penguin)

- **Reading Magic: Why Reading Aloud to Our Children Will Change Their Lives Forever,** by Mem Fox (Harcourt)

- **Read to Me: Raising Kids Who Love to Read,** by Bernice Cullinan (Scholastic)

- **Parents Are Teachers, Too,** by Claudia Jones (Williamson)

- **Hey! Listen to This: Stories to Read-Aloud,** by Jim Trelease (Penguin)

- **Let's Read About . . . Finding Books They'll Love to Read,** by Bernice Cullinan (Scholastic)

- **Michele Landsberg's Guide to Children's Books,** by Michele Landsberg (Penguin)

- **A Parent's Guide to Children's Reading,** by Nancy Larrick (Bantam)

- **The Hurried Child: Growing Up Too Fast Too Soon, 3d ed.,** by David Elkind (Perseus Publishing)

Web Sites

- **www.trelease-on-reading.com**—Web site of Jim Trelease, author of *The New Read-Aloud Handbook* (Penguin)

- **www.ala.org/booklist/**—Lists of notable children's books arranged by age group

- **gpn.unl.edu/rainbow**—*Reading Rainbow* site; includes a listing of all the books covered on its episodes since the program's inception

Children's Book Corner: A READ-ALOUD Resource with Tips, Techniques, and Plans for Teachers, Librarians, and Parents, by Judy Bradbury. Westport, CT: Libraries Unlimited, 2004

- **www.readingrockets.org**—A friendly site with all sorts of information that is helpful to parents as well as teachers and librarians, this is a national service of public television station WETA in Washington, D.C.

To Purchase Books Online

- **www.amazon.com**

- **www.barnesandnoble.com**

And Last But Not Least . . .

Public and school librarians and classroom teachers, of course!

Children's Book Corner: A READ-ALOUD Resource with Tips, Techniques, and Plans for Teachers, Librarians, and Parents, by Judy Bradbury. Westport, CT: Libraries Unlimited, 2004

Raising Readers

Tips and Techniques for Parents

by Judy Bradbury

WHAT IS THE CALDECOTT AWARD?

Established in 1938, the **Caldecott Award** is given yearly to the illustrator of "the most distinguished contribution" to literature for children published in the United States during the previous year. It is named for Randolph J. Caldecott, an English illustrator whose work represented the "joyousness of picture books as well as their beauty." **Caldecott Honors** are also awarded.

While not the only measure of a worthwhile choice for young children, Caldecott Medal books are hallmarks of quality in books for children. Listed below are selected titles especially appropriate for first and second graders.

Selected Caldecott Award Winners

- 2000: JOSEPH HAD AN OVERCOAT, by Simms Taback (Viking)

- 1998: RAPUNZEL, by Paul O. Zelinsky (Dutton)

- 1996: OFFICER BUCKLE AND GLORIA, by Peggy Rathmann (Putnam)

- 1993: MIRETTE ON THE HIGH WIRE, by Emily Arnold McCully (Putnam)

- 1994: GRANDFATHER'S JOURNEY, by Allen Say (Houghton Mifflin)

- 1990: LON PO PO: A RED RIDING HOOD STORY FROM CHINA, by Ed Young (Philomel)

- 1989: SONG AND DANCE MAN, illustrated by Stephen Gammell and written by Karen Ackerman (Knopf)

- 1988: OWL MOON, illustrated by John Schoenherr and written by Jane Yolen (Philomel)

- 1986: THE POLAR EXPRESS, by Chris Van Allsburg (Houghton Mifflin)

- 1981: FABLES, by Arnold Lobel (HarperCollins)

- 1980: OX-CART MAN, illustrated by Barbara Cooney and written by Donald Hall (Viking)

- 1976: WHY MOSQUITOES BUZZ IN PEOPLE'S EARS illustrated by Leo and Diane Dillon; translated by Verna Aardema; Dial

- 1970: SYLVESTER AND THE MAGIC PEBBLE by William Steig; Aladdin

Children's Book Corner: A READ-ALOUD Resource with Tips, Techniques, and Plans for Teachers, Librarians, and Parents, by Judy Bradbury. Westport, CT: Libraries Unlimited, 2004

Raising Readers

Tips and Techniques for Parents

by Judy Bradbury

IT'S A SPOON, NOT A SHOVEL

And Other Books About Manners Especially for Six- to Eight-Year-Olds

It's amazing how that child you're grooming for greatness can't seem to figure out how to chew with his (or her) mouth closed. And when you gently bring the lapse to your cherub's attention, he shrugs as if that's the last thing in the world you should care a whit about.

As with other trials of parenthood, when all else fails, try humor. You can probably gather from the titles listed below (and above) that there's a pile of engaging books that introduce the rules of etiquette in a way that will appeal to your wayward prince or princess. Hopefully, your dear child will swallow that mouthful of pizza before laughing out loud . . . .

- IT'S A SPOON, NOT A SHOVEL, written by Caralyn Buehner and illustrated by Mark Buehner (Puffin). Great title, super illustrations of situations that may be silly but nevertheless get the message across. See also I DID IT, I'M SORRY; multiple choice questions follow anecdotes. Answers are found on the last page.

- EXCUSE ME!, by Lisa Kopelke (Simon & Schuster). A burping frog's problem gets bigger and badder until he remembers his manners.

- MANNERS, by Aliki (HarperCollins); simple rules of etiquette. See also COMMUNICATION, about talking and listening, by the same author/illustrator.

- PERFECT PIGS, written by Marc Brown and illustrated by Stephen Krensky (Little, Brown). The title says it all.

- THE ANT AND THE ELEPHANT, by Bill Peet (Houghton Mifflin). Listeners learn about gratitude in this story about an elephant who helps a number of ungrateful slugs out of a jam.

- MY DOG NEVER SAYS PLEASE, written by Suzanne Williams and illustrated by Tedd Arnold (Penguin). Manners are such a bother. Is it be easier to be a dog?

- WE LIVE HERE TOO! KIDS TALK ABOUT GOOD CITIZENSHIP, written by Nancy Loewen and illustrated by Omarr Wesley (Picture Window Books); inviting, humorous advice column format; discusses acting responsibly.

Children's Book Corner: A READ-ALOUD Resource with Tips, Techniques, and Plans for Teachers, Librarians, and Parents, by Judy Bradbury. Westport, CT: Libraries Unlimited, 2004

Raising Readers

Tips and Techniques for Parents

by Judy Bradbury

MAGICAL MATH BOOKS MAKE "BOR-R-RING!" DISAPPEAR

Especially for Six- to Eight-Year-Olds

Does math muddle your youngster's mind? Would she rather empty the garbage than tackle a sheet full of numbers? Is math homework work for you?

The books listed below give math new life and a new image. They demonstrate in an entertaining way that math is all around us, and it's not something to dread. Meant to be read aloud or read alone, these books are sure to please your child and help him view math in a new light. For those children who are nimble with numbers, they're perfect reads, too, because they reinforce the fun you can have finessing figures. Really!

- MATH-TERPIECES, written by Greg Tang and illustrated by Greg Paprocki (Scholastic). Math and art masterpieces meet in the middle!

- MATH FOR ALL SEASONS, written by Greg Tang and illustrated by Harry Briggs (Scholastic); math riddle-rhymes on addition, subtracting to add, and patterns.

- THE DOORBELL RANG, by Pat Hutchins (Greenwillow); cookies and division.

- ONE CARTON OF OOPS!, written by Judy Bradbury and illustrated by Cathy Trachok (McGraw-Hill). Christopher is sent to the store for a carton of eggs and his troubles begin; concept of a dozen; subtraction.

- DOUBLE BUBBLE TROUBLE!, written by Judy Bradbury and illustrated by Cathy Trachok (McGraw-Hill). Christopher gets in trouble for chewing gum in class, but finds a way to blow his troubles away; counting by twos.

- THE FLY ON THE CEILING A MATH MYTH, written by Dr. Julie Glass and illustrated by Richard Walz (Random House); graphing and coordinates.

- THE CASE OF THE MISSING BIRTHDAY PARTY, written by Joanne Rocklin and illustrated by John Speirs (Scholastic); digits and place value.

- A HIGH-FIVING GIFT FOR MOM!, written by Judy Bradbury and illustrated by Cathy Trachok (McGraw-Hill). A teacher's craft fair offers lots of options; money.

Children's Book Corner: A READ-ALOUD Resource with Tips, Techniques, and Plans for Teachers, Librarians, and Parents, by Judy Bradbury. Westport, CT: Libraries Unlimited, 2004

- HOW MUCH IS THAT GUINEA PIG IN THE WINDOW?, written by Joanne Rocklin and illustrated by Meredith Johnson (Scholastic); money, addition, multiplication, calculation.

- HOW MUCH IS A MILLION?, written by David M. Schwartz and illustrated by Steven Kellogg (HarperCollins); explains a million, a billion, and a trillion.

- EATING FRACTIONS, by Bruce McMillan (Scholastic); with photographs.

- DOGGONE LEMONADE STAND!, written by Judy Bradbury and illustrated by Cathy Trachok (McGraw-Hill); a dog and a lemonade stand on the hottest day of the year; simple fractions.

- THE PHILHARMONIC GETS DRESSED, written by Karla Kuskin and illustrated by Marc Simont (HarperCollins); math and musicians meet.

- MATH CURSE, written by Jon Scieszka and illustrated by Lane Smith (Viking); zany, zesty, zippy fun.

- ALEXANDER, WHO USED TO BE RICH LAST SUNDAY, written by Judith Viorst and illustrated by Ray Cruz (Aladdin). There's so much you could do with a dollar!

Children's Book Corner: A READ-ALOUD Resource with Tips, Techniques, and Plans for Teachers, Librarians, and Parents, by Judy Bradbury. Westport, CT: Libraries Unlimited, 2004

Raising Readers

Tips and Techniques for Parents

by Judy Bradbury

THE MIGHTY PEN

Books about the Power of the Written Word Suitable for Six- to Eight-Year-Olds

Reinforce the value of being able to put thoughts on paper by reading aloud the entertaining books listed below with your child.

- CLICK, CLACK, MOO, COWS THAT TYPE, written by Doreen Cronin and illustrated by Betsy Lewin (Simon & Schuster). The barnyard organizer puts his demands in writing.

- DEAR MRS. LARUE: LETTERS FROM OBEDIENCE SCHOOL, by Mark Teague (Scholastic). A dog's correspondence details his incarceration for his master.

- ANGELINA BALLERINA'S INVITATION TO THE BALLET, written by Katharine Holabird and illustrated by Helen Craig (Pleasant Company); includes pull out letters and poster.

- THE JOLLY POSTMAN OR OTHER PEOPLE'S LETTERS, by Janet and Allan Ahlberg (Little, Brown); pull-out letters from fairy tale characters. See also THE JOLLY POCKET POSTMAN and THE JOLLY CHRISTMAS POSTMAN.

- DEAR ANNIE, by Judith Caseley (Greenwillow). Letters between a girl and her grandfather chronicle her childhood.

- BEETHOVEN LIVES UPSTAIRS, written by Barbara Nichol and illustrated by Scott Cameron (Orchard Books); letters to uncle about one famous boarder.

- FREDERICK, by Leo Lionni (Random House). A mouse's lyrical words lighten and brighten dreary winter for his field mice friends.

- PUNCTUATION TAKES A VACATION, written by Robin Pulver and illustrated by Lynn Rowe Reed (Holiday House). The punctuation marks have had it!

- THE AMAZING POP-UP GRAMMAR BOOK, by Jennie Maizels and Kate Petty (Dutton). A book that lives up to its name.

- THE GARDENER, written by Sarah Stewart and illustrated by David Small (Farrar, Straus & Giroux); Caldecott Honor; set during the Depression, a girl writes home.

Children's Book Corner: A READ-ALOUD Resource with Tips, Techniques, and Plans for Teachers, Librarians, and Parents, by Judy Bradbury. Westport, CT: Libraries Unlimited, 2004

Raising Readers

Tips and Techniques for Parents

by Judy Bradbury

BOOKS ABOUT DEATH FOR CHILDREN SUITABLE FOR SIX- TO EIGHT-YEAR-OLDS

When a child is confronted with the death of a loved one, it can be overwhelming—to the parent as well as the child. Death is never easy to explain, and trying to ease the pain of little ones can be heartrending for grieving parents or caregivers. Following is a list of books that sensitively address this difficult subject with compassion, insight, gentleness, and wisdom.

- NANA UPSTAIRS & NANA DOWNSTAIRS, by Tomie dePaola (Putnam); the love between a child and a grandparent, and learning about and accepting death.

- GARDEN ANGEL, written by Jan M. Czech and illustrated by Susan Aitken (Centering Corporation). A child plants a garden as she used to with her grandfather.

- MY GRANDSON LEW, written by Charlotte Zolotow and illustrated by William Pene du Bois (HarperCollins). Lewis and his mother remember together a man they both miss.

- THE TENTH GOOD THING ABOUT BARNEY, written by Judith Viorst and illustrated by Erik Blegvad (Atheneum); about the loss of a cat.

- I'LL ALWAYS LOVE YOU, by Hans Wilhelm (Crown); the loss of a pet dog and the lessons it brings.

Children's Book Corner: A READ-ALOUD Resource with Tips, Techniques, and Plans for Teachers, Librarians, and Parents, by Judy Bradbury. Westport, CT: Libraries Unlimited, 2004

Raising Readers

Tips and Techniques for Parents

by Judy Bradbury

CHAPTER BOOKS TO READ ALOUD ESPECIALLY SUITABLE FOR SIX- TO EIGHT-YEAR-OLDS

Listed below are selected, well-loved chapter book series perfect for reading aloud to first and second graders. They're certain to enrapture the listener as well as the adult who reads them aloud!

The Littles: A treasury of tales written by John Peterson and illustrated by Roberta Carter Clark about a family six inches tall with tails (Scholastic).

THE LITTLES

THE LITTLES AND THE BIG STORM

THE LITTLES AND THE TRASH TINIES

THE LITTLES TO THE RESCUE

THE LITTLES GO TO SCHOOL

THE LITTLES GIVE A PARTY

THE LITTLES AND THE LOST CHILDREN

TOM LITTLE'S GREAT HALLOWEEN SCARE

Mrs. Piggle-Wiggle: A character children will love who smells like cookies, lives in an upside-down house, and was once married to a pirate! But best of all, she helps children in her neighborhood overcome any problems, from hating baths to eating too slowly. Pure delight, fine fun; written by Betty MacDonald and illustrated by Hilary Knight (with the exception of FARM, which was illustrated by Maurice Sendak) (HarperCollins).

MRS. PIGGLE-WIGGLE

MRS. PIGGLE-WIGGLE'S MAGIC

MRS. PIGGLE WIGGLE'S FARM

HELLO, MRS. PIGGLE-WIGGLE

The Hilarious Adventures of Paddington: Who doesn't recognize the adorable bear with the yellow hat and blue overcoat with the tag attached that reads,

Children's Book Corner: A READ-ALOUD Resource with Tips, Techniques, and Plans for Teachers, Librarians, and Parents, by Judy Bradbury. Westport, CT: Libraries Unlimited, 2004

"Please look after this BEAR thank you." Sweet, humorous, gentle tales written by Michael Bond with illustrations by Peggy Fortnum (Dell).

A BEAR CALLED PADDINGTON

MORE ABOUT PADDINGTON

PADDINGTON HELPS OUT

PADDINGTON AT LARGE

PADDINGTON AT WORK

PADDINGTON ABROAD

PADDINGTON MARCHES ON

My Father's Dragon: A trilogy written by Ruth Stiles Gannett and illustrated by Ruth Chrisman Gannett (Random House). The first of these books of pure silliness paired with adventure is about a boy's trip to Wild Island to save a dragon, and was awarded a Newbery Honor. This set of books has been winning the hearts and imaginations of children since it was first published in 1948.

MY FATHER'S DRAGON

ELMER AND THE DRAGON

THE DRAGONS OF BLUELAND

The Spiderwick Chronicles: A new series that will be five books in all, by an award-winning team that has garnered much interest as a solid choice for fantasy lovers who can't quite tackle (or lift) the Harry Potter series; by Tony DiTerlizzi and Holly Black (Simon & Schuster).

THE FIELD GUIDE

THE SEEING STONE

LUCINDA'S SECRET

Children's Book Corner: A READ-ALOUD Resource with Tips, Techniques, and Plans for Teachers, Librarians, and Parents, by Judy Bradbury. Westport, CT: Libraries Unlimited, 2004

Raising Readers

Tips and Techniques for Parents

by Judy Bradbury

CHAPTER BOOKS FOR BEGINNING READERS TO READ ON THEIR OWN

Listed below are selected paperback chapter books written and published with the newly independent reader in mind. Typically 48 pages in length, they are colorful, inexpensive, and typically smaller in size than most picture books. They're written in simple, short chapters. The print is large, and there's lots of space around the words. Illustrations are often black-and-white line drawings that aid comprehension and make the book inviting to young readers.

Beginning chapter books bridge the gap from picture books to more complex chapter books. Levels are indicated on the cover for the convenience of teachers and parents. A page of pointers for adults is often included.

Some classic beginning readers are 40 years old or more! New series and new titles are released regularly. Listed below are some of the best books for beginning readers to read on their own.

Hello Reader! Series: These single-title books make up a library of their own. Published by Scholastic, there are four levels from preschool through grade 3.

I Can Read It All By Myself Beginner Books: These are Random House books, many of which were written by Dr. Seuss, with titles you most likely knew as a child, such as THE CAT IN THE HAT, HOP ON POP, and THE FOOT BOOK.

STEP Into Reading: Published by Random House, there are four levels in this series, offering a variety of books on many subjects.

I Can Read Books: Recently redesigned, this series published by HarperCollins, boasts five levels from preschool to simple chapter books. Authors, illustrators, and topics vary. Classics include FROG AND TOAD, AMELIA BEDELIA, DANNY AND THE DINOSAUR, and LITTLE BEAR.

Let's-Read-and-Find-Out Science: Listed as one of the top 10 nonfiction series by the American Library Association, these leveled books published by HarperCollins present science concepts in a colorful, engaging manner.

Oliver and Amanda Pig Books: Written by Jean Van Leeuwen and illustrated by Arnold Lobel. They chronicle the humorous and memorable everyday events of Oliver and his younger sister, Amanda. (Puffin Easy-to-Read Program).

Children's Book Corner: A READ-ALOUD Resource with Tips, Techniques, and Plans for Teachers, Librarians, and Parents, by Judy Bradbury. Westport, CT: Libraries Unlimited, 2004

Morris and Boris Books: This wacky duo—one bear, one moose—could easily have invented slapstick; by Bernard Wiseman (Penguin).

Henry and Mudge Series: Kids love Henry and his big dog, Mudge. Written by Cynthia Rylant and illustrated by Sucie Stevenson (and more recently Carolyn Bracken "in the style of Sucie Stevenson") , this series has won numerous accolades and sold millions of copies (Simon & Schuster Ready-to-Read).

WHY CAN'T I FLY?: Minnie the monkey wants to learn to fly. She tries and she tries. "I can fly, I can fly, I can . . . flop," she says over and over until her friends help. By Rita Golden Gelman, illustrated by Jack Kent (Scholastic).

SLEEPING UGLY: Written by Jane Yolen and illustrated by Diane Stanley (Putnam). Princess Miserella is beautiful and mean, while Plain Jane is kind but has "a face to match her name." Humorous delivery of wishes and a healthy dose of misunderstanding will make this book a favorite.

THE BLUE RIBBON PUPPIES: Classic by Crockett Johnson, author of HAROLD AND THE PURPLE CRAYON (HarperCollins); the story of how a boy and girl decide who should get the blue ribbons among seven pups.

THE CARROT SEED: Written by Ruth Krauss and illustrated by Crockett Johnson with sunny yellow pages; a perfect springtime book for beginning readers (HarperCollins).

THE HORSE IN HARRY'S ROOM: The story of Harry and his imaginary horse, by Syd Hoff (HarperCollins).

PEARL AND WAGNER TWO GOOD FRIENDS: A three-chapter book written by Kate McMullen and illustrated by R. W. Alley, who aptly depicts the companionship and comical repartee that transpire between this rabbit and mouse, two good friends and two great characters (Dial).

THE LITTLE FISH THAT GOT AWAY: First published in 1956 by David McKay Company,; written by Bernadine Cook and illustrated by Crockett Johnson; a delightful chronicle of a boy's experience fishing. Giggles guaranteed.

Children's Book Corner: A READ-ALOUD Resource with Tips, Techniques, and Plans for Teachers, Librarians, and Parents, by Judy Bradbury. Westport, CT: Libraries Unlimited, 2004

Raising Readers

Tips and Techniques for Parents

by Judy Bradbury

CHAPTER BOOKS FOR INDEPENDENT READERS TO READ ON THEIR OWN

Has your child exhausted the shelf of beginning readers? Is your reader ready to graduate to the next level? Listed below are longer chapter books just right for children reading on a second-grade level. Find them at your local library or bookstore. Need a gift? Here's your list!

AGAPANTHUS HUM AND THE EYEGLASSES; AGAPANTHUS HUM AND THE ANGEL HOOT: Written by Joy Cowley and illustrated by Jennifer Plecas (Philomel); humorous chapter books about a "whizzy, dizzy" gal and her friends.

THE STORIES JULIAN TELLS; MORE STORIES JULIAN TELLS: By Ann Cameron (Knopf). Julian likes to tell stories: tall, tall tales that get him into a heap of trouble. Related titles are also available.

GOONEY BIRD GREENE: Written by Newbery winner Lois Lowry and illustrated by Middy Thomas (Houghton Mifflin). A most unusual free spirit joins a memorably typical second-grade class, and nobody is the same from the moment she sets foot in the door.

THE HERO OF THIRD GRADE: Written by Alice DeLaCroix and illustrated by Cynthia Fisher (Holiday House). A new town, newly divorced parents, a new school in April: Is Randall's life ruined, or will he become a hero on the order of the Scarlet Pimpernel? For more accomplished readers.

Hopscotch Hill School Series: Written by Valerie Tripp and illustrated by Joy Allen (Pleasant Company) (American Girl). Each book focuses on one child in Hopscotch Hill School; includes "Dear Parents" notes and activities.

Horrible Harry Series: This rascal will keep kids giggling: and reading; several titles, including HORRIBLE HARRY IN ROOM 2B and HORRIBLE HARRY AND THE ANT INVASION; by Suzy Kline (Viking).

Magic Tree House Series: Fantasies by Mary Pope Osborne; titles include DINOSAURS BEFORE DARK and PIRATES PAST NOON (Random House).

Children's Book Corner: A READ-ALOUD Resource with Tips, Techniques, and Plans for Teachers, Librarians, and Parents, by Judy Bradbury. Westport, CT: Libraries Unlimited, 2004

The Kids of the Polk Street School Series: A library of titles written by teacher, reading consultant, and award-winning author Patricia Reilly Giff. Higher second-grade level (Dell). See also Polka Dot Private Eye series.

Marvin Redpost Series: By Louis Sachar (HOLES) (Random House); funny stories about the misadventures of a third-grade boy with an imagination.

The Cam Jansen Series: YOUNG CAM JANSEN and CAM JANSEN; titles for beginning and advancing readers in grades 1 and 2–3 respectively, written by David A. Adler (Viking); about Cam, who has a photographic memory. Published by Scholastic; copyright Waddingtons Games Ltd.

Clue Jr. Series: Created by Parker C. Hinter; based on the board game; offers simple cases for readers to solve. Solutions at the end of each chapter.

Amber Brown Series: A contemporary third grader with realistic problems and believable friends, Amber is funny, feisty, and popular among independent readers of advanced second- and beginning third-grade level; by Paula Danziger. Published in hardcover by Putnam and in paperback by Apple Books/Scholastic.

Riverside Kids Series: by Johanna Hurwitz; numerous books suitable for readers on a mid-second-grade level. Titles include BUSYBODY NORA, E IS FOR ELISA, and RIP-ROARING RUSSELL. Published by HarperCollins.

Third-Grade Detectives Series: Interactive in style, these stories encourage the reader to solve cases that teacher and former spy, Mr. Merlin, presents to his students; written by George E. Stanley. Published by Aladdin.

The Matt Christopher Series: The "#1 Sports series for kids" according to publisher Little, Brown. Numerous titles.

Children's Book Corner: A READ-ALOUD Resource with Tips, Techniques, and Plans for Teachers, Librarians, and Parents, by Judy Bradbury. Westport, CT: Libraries Unlimited, 2004

Book Notes

An Annotated Listing of Read-Aloud Titles
Especially for Six- to Eight-Year-Olds

Listed here are hundreds of books especially suitable for reading aloud to six- to eight-year-olds. They are categorized by subject and briefly described to help teachers, librarians, and parents find just the right book to share with that special child or group of children. Bibliographic information is included for each title.

HOLIDAYS AND SEASONS OF THE YEAR

Winter

- KATY AND THE BIG SNOW, by Virginia Lee Burton (Houghton Mifflin); a classic about a red tractor that plows snow.

- THOMAS' SNOWSUIT, written by Robert Munsch and illustrated by Michael Martchenko (Annick Press); a wacky story about what ensues when Thomas rebels against wearing his snowsuit.

- SNOWMEN AT NIGHT, written by Caralyn Buehner and illustrated by Mark Buehner (Dial); the escapades of snowmen who cavort while we sleep; fabulous art.

- ANNA, GRANPA, AND THE BIG STORM, written by Carla Stevens and illustrated by Margot Thomas (Clarion); a chapter book in which a girl and her grandfather get caught in the Great Blizzard of 1888 en route to a spelling bee.

- WINTER POEMS, selected by Barbara Rogasky and illustrated by Trina Schart Hyman (Scholastic); 25 poems from Shakespeare to Sandburg to Japanese haiku celebrate the season.

- THE BIG SNOW, by Berta and Elmer Hader (Aladdin); Caldecott classic.

- WHITE SNOW, BRIGHT SNOW, illustrated by Robert Duvoisin and written by Alvin Tresselt (HarperCollins); another Caldecott classic.

- GOODBYE GEESE, written by Nancy White Carlstrom and illustrated by Ed Young (Philomel); lyrical and lovely.

- SADIE AND THE SNOWMAN, written by Allen Morgan and illustrated by Brenda Clark (Kids Can Press); Sadie saves her snowman.

- THANK YOU, SANTA, written by Margaret Wild and illustrated by Kerry Argent (Omnibus Books); letters throughout the year between a girl and Santa.

- OWL MOON, written by Jane Yolen and illustrated by John Schoenherr (Philomel); see the read-aloud plan in *Children's Book Corner, Pre-K–K*.

Groundhog Day

- IT'S GROUNDHOG DAY!, written by Steven Kroll and illustrated by Jeni Bassett (Holiday House); sweet fun with facts about the day.

Valentine's Day

- FOUR VALENTINES IN A RAINSTORM, by Felicia Bond (HarperCollins); a perfect picture book.

- IT'S VALENTINE'S DAY, poems by Jack Prelutsky and illustrated by Yossi Abolafia (HarperCollins); a nonfattening treat for this holiday.

- THE VALENTINE CAT, written by Clyde Robert Bulla and illustrated by Leonard Weisgard (Troll); a classic tale in which a kitten helps a man find his way back to joy.

- MY BOOK OF FUNNY VALENTINES, written by Margo Lundell and illustrated by Nate Evans (Scholastic); silly poems.

- ROSES ARE PINK, YOUR FEET REALLY STINK, by Diane de Groat (HarperCollins). Gilbert writes naughty and nice poems on his Valentine's Day cards.

St. Patrick's Day

- CLEVER TOM AND THE LEPRECHAUN, retold and illustrated by Linda Shute (HarperCollins); folk tale.

Easter

- BUNNY TROUBLE and BAD, BAD BUNNY TROUBLE, by Hans Wilhelm (Scholastic); starring Ralph, the bunny that would rather play soccer than do anything else.

- CHICKEN SUNDAY, by Patricia Polacco (Philomel); Children's Choice and ALA Notable Book about differences, friendship, and character.

- EASTER BUDS ARE SPRINGING POEMS FOR EASTER, selected by Lee Bennett Hopkins and illustrated by Tomie de Paola (Boyds Mills Press).

- MAX'S CHOCOLATE CHICKEN, by Rosemary Wells (Dial). Sly Max outwits his older sister Ruby.

Mother's Day

- THE MOTHER'S DAY MICE, written by Eve Bunting and illustrated by Jan Brett (Clarion); see the read-aloud plan.

- HAPPY MOTHER'S DAY, written by Steven Kroll and illustrated by Marylin Hafner (Holiday House). A big family with a big heart plans a special day for mom.

- A HIGH-FIVING GIFT FOR MOM!, written by Judy Bradbury and illustrated by Cathy Trachok (McGraw-Hill). Christopher and his brothers go to a teachers' craft fair to buy a gift for Mother's Day.

Father's Day

- A PERFECT FATHER'S DAY, written by Eve Bunting and illustrated by Susan Meddaugh (Clarion). A girl and her dad celebrate Father's Day doing her favorite things, and on the last page it's Dad's turn.

Summer

- TAR BEACH, by Faith Ringgold (Crown); Coretta Scott King Award for Illustration; Caldecott Honor; a girl, her dreams, and her rooftop beach.

- SHOOTING STAR SUMMER, written by Candice F. Ransom and illustrated by Karen Milone (Boyds Mills Press). A dreaded visit from a cousin proves memorable.

- ANNA'S GARDEN SONGS, poems by Mary Q. Steele and illustrated by Lena Anderson (HarperCollins).

- ANNA'S SUMMER SONGS, poems by Mary Q. Steele and illustrated by Lena Anderson (HarperCollins).

- THE SUN, THE WIND AND THE RAIN, written by Lisa Westberg Peters and illustrated by Ted Rand (Holt). Basic geology concepts parallel a story about a day at the beach building a sandcastle.

- BLUEBERRIES FOR SAL, by Robert McCloskey (Penguin); a classic.

- DOGGONE LEMONADE STAND!, written by Judy Bradbury and illustrated by Cathy Trachok (McGraw-Hill). Christopher sets up a lemonade stand on the hottest day of the year; simple fractions.

Fall/Halloween

- PUMPKIN JACK, written and illustrated by Will Hubbell (Whitman). A pumpkin grows from the remains of last year's jack-o'-lantern placed in the yard.

- THE LITTLE OLD LADY WHO WAS NOT AFRAID OF ANYTHING, written by Linda Williams and illustrated by Megan Lloyd (HarperCollins); lively, cumulative story with a catchy refrain, evocative language, an endearing character, a bit of a scare, and a reassuring ending.

- ROOM ON THE BROOM, written by Julia Donaldson and illustrated by Axel Scheffler (Dial); by the team who created THE GRUFFALO (see *Children's Book Corner Pre-K–K* for the read-aloud plan), this rhyming tale about friendship and quick wit is a Halloween hoot.

- FIVE FUNNY FRIGHTS, written by Judith Bauer Stamper and illustrated by Tim Raglin (Scholastic); a Hello Reader title of five funny, short Halloween tales.

- BEAST AND THE HALLOWEEN HORROR, written by Patricia Reilly Giff and illustrated by Blanche Sims (Dell); chapter book about one of the characters of the Polk Street School, a series by the Newbery Honor Award-winning author, teacher, and reading consultant. In this installment, Beast, for whom school is a bit of a challenge, writes a letter to an author about how much he loved the dog in his book. Only there was no dog and now the author is coming to Beast's school for Halloween!

- TOM LITTLE'S GREAT HALLOWEEN SCARE, written by John Peterson and illustrated by Roberta Carter Clark (Scholastic). Lucy saves the day when Tom's idea for a Halloween prank goes awry; from the classic best-selling series of tales about the miniature family with tails.

- IT'S HALLOWEEN, poems by Jack Prelutsky and illustrated by Marylin Hafner (HarperCollins); pure Prelutsky humor in verse.

- HIST WHIST, written by e.e. cummings and illustrated by Deborah Kogan Ray (Crown); exquisitely illustrated poem.

Thanksgiving

- THANKSGIVING AT THE TAPPLETONS', written by Eileen Spinelli and illustrated by Maryann Cocca-Leffler (HarperCollins); see the read-aloud plan.

- A PLUMP AND PERKY TURKEY, written by Teresa Bateman and illustrated by Jeff Shelly (Scholastic); rhymed text in which Pete, a perky turkey, eludes the townspeople of Squawk Valley and proves that this bird sometimes can be "pretty doggone clever."

- SARAH MORTON'S DAY: A DAY IN THE LIFE OF A PILGRIM GIRL, written by Kate Winters, with photographs by Russ Kendall (Scholastic). The story takes place in 1627. Photographed at Plimoth Plantation, Cape Cod; see the read-aloud plan.

- SAMUEL EATON'S DAY: A DAY IN THE LIFE OF A PILGRIM BOY, written by Kate Winters, with photographs by Russ Kendall (Scholastic); companion to the previous book.

- ON THE MAYFLOWER: VOYAGE OF THE SHIP'S APPRENTICE & A PASSENGER GIRL, written by Kate Winters, with photographs by Russ Kendall (Scholastic); companion to the two previous books.

- TURKEY TROUBLE, written by Patricia Reilly Giff and illustrated by Blanche Sims (Dell); a Polk Street Special featuring Emily Arrow, a student in Mrs. Rooney's class; includes recipes and crafts.

Christmas

- THE FEATHERED CROWN, written by Marsha Hayles and illustrated by Bernadette Pons (Holt); lilting rhyme; mother birds journey to make a bed for baby Jesus.

- THE JOLLY CHRISTMAS POSTMAN, by Janet Ahlberg and Allan Ahlberg (Little, Brown); letters and cards lift from envelope pages.

- LITTLE TREE, written by e.e. cummings and illustrated by Deborah Kogan Ray (Crown); a Christmas poem illustrated with dreamy paintings.

- THE POLAR EXPRESS, by Chris Van Allsburg (Houghton Mifflin); see the read-aloud plan.

- ANGELINA'S CHRISTMAS, written by Katharine Holabird and illustrated by Helen Craig (Random House). Angelina shares Christmas with a lonely postman.

- CHRISTMAS WITH MORRIS AND BORIS, by Bernard Wiseman (Little, Brown); beginning reader; hee-haw humor.

- MERRY CHRISTMAS, AMELIA BEDELIA, written by Peggy Parish and illustrated by Lynn Sweat (Greenwillow); beginning reader featuring wacky housekeeper.

- THE PUPPY WHO WANTED A BOY, written by Jane Thayer and illustrated by Lisa McCue (HarperCollins). A puppy wants a boy for Christmas.

- ONLY A STAR, written by Margery Facklam and illustrated by Nancy Carpenter (Eerdmans); spotlights the creatures that lived in the Holy Land at the time of Jesus's birth; nonfiction; rhyming text; breathtaking illustrations.

- A MOON IN MY TEACUP, by Anita Riggio (Boyds Mills Press); nostalgic oil paintings; the manger scene stirs special feelings on a visit to Grandma and Grandpa's house.

- THE FRIENDLY BEASTS, illustrated by Tomie dePaola (Putnam); old English Christmas carol.

- THE CHRISTMAS MIRACLE OF JONATHAN TOOMEY, written by Susan Wojciechowski and illustrated by P. J. Lynch (Candlewick). A widow, her son, and a sad woodcarver make for joy and a miracle.

- SANTA CALLS, by William Joyce (HarperCollins); a Christmas fantasy unlike any other.

- FATHER CHRISTMAS, by Raymond Briggs (Puffin). Follow the man on his longest work night of the year.

- NUTCRACKER NOEL, written by Kate McMullan and illustrated by Jim McMullan (HarperCollins). Noel makes lemons from lemonade in her role as a tree in the *Nutcracker.*

- THE LITTLE DRUMMER BOY, words and music by Katherine Davis, Henry Onorati, and Harry Simeone; illustrated by Ezra Jack Keats (Macmillan).

- IT'S CHRISTMAS, poems by Jack Prelutsky and illustrated by Marylin Hafner (Greenwillow); silly, fun, re-readable.

- THE STORY OF THE NUTCRACKER BALLET, written by Deborah Hautzig and illustrated by Diane Goode (Random House).

- MIRACLE ON 34TH STREET, written by Valentine Davies and illustrated by Tomie dePaola (Harcourt); an illustrated chapter book of the classic Christmas story.

- ZELDA AND IVY ONE CHRISTMAS, by Laura McGee Kvasnosky (Candlewick); a short chapter book in the series about these endearing sisters.

Hanukkah

- THE BORROWED HANUKKAH LATKES, written by Linda Glaser and illustrated by Nancy Cote (Whitman); see the read-aloud plan.

- CHANUKAH LIGHTS EVERYWHERE, written by Michael J. Rosen and illustrated by Melissa Iwai (Harcourt). A young boy contemplates the lights on his menorah and in the world around him.

- INSIDE-OUT GRANDMA A HANUKKAH STORY, by Joan Rothenberg (Hyperion); a delightful cumulative story; includes a recipe for latkes.

- A PICTURE BOOK OF HANUKKAH, written by David A. Adler and illustrated by Linda Heller (Holiday House); nonfiction.

- THE FIRST NIGHT OF HANUKKAH, written and illustrated by Nicki Weiss (Grosset & Dunlap); an All Aboard Reading Level 2 beginning reader; tells the story of the miracle of the oil.

- SAMMY SPIDER'S FIRST HANUKKAH, written by Sylvia A. Rouss and illustrated by Katherine Janus Kahn (Kar-Ben Copies). A spider experiences Hanukkah from the ceiling above; also colors and numbers.

- LATKES AND APPLESAUCE A HANUKKAH STORY, written by Fran Manushkin and illustrated by Robin Spowart (Scholastic); a Blue Ribbon Book.

- HANUKKAH HA-HAS KNOCK-KNOCK JOKES THAT ARE A LATKE FUN, written by Katy Hall and Lisa Eisenberg and illustrated by Stephen Carpenter (HarperCollins); lift-the-flap knock-knock jokes.

- THE EIGHT NIGHTS OF HANUKKAH, written by Judy Nayer and illustrated by Yuri Salzman (Creative Media Applications; Troll); history, activities, story, and song.

- WHEN MINDY SAVED HANUKKAH, written by Eric A. Kimmel and illustrated by Barbara McClintock (Scholastic). A miniature Jewish family must outwit a cat in order to get candles for the menorah.

- HANUKKAH LIGHTS, HANUKKAH NIGHTS, written by Leslie Kimmelman and illustrated by John Himmelman (HarperCollins). Press the button to hear music for "My Little Dreidel"; also a story.

- THE CHANUKKAH GUEST, written by Eric A. Kimmel and illustrated by Giora Carmi (Holiday House). Nearsighted, 97-year-old Bubba Brayna shares the holiday with a bear she mistakes for the rabbi.

- JEREMY'S DREIDEL, written by Ellie Gellman and illustrated by Judith Friedman (Kar-Ben Copies). Jeremy makes a Braille dreidel for his father, who is blind.

- THE JAR OF FOOLS EIGHT HANUKKAH STORIES FROM CHELM, by Eric A. Kimmel and illustrated by Mordicai Gerstein (Holiday House). "Chelm is the traditional town of fools . . . [who] are not stupid . . . unfortunately they are nearly always wrong," according to notes by the author.

- THE MAGIC MENORAH A MODERN CHANUKAH TALE, written by Jane Breskin Zalben and illustrated by Donna Diamond (Simon & Schuster); an early chapter book. Stanley shines the shammash and poof! just like a genie, an old man appears.

- HANUKKAH!, written by Roni Schotter and illustrated by Marylin Hafner (Little, Brown); simple story with delightful illustrations about a family celebrating the holiday.

Kwanzaa

- THE GIFTS OF KWANZAA, by Synthia Saint James (Whitman). Bold illustrations accompany clear explanations of the seven principles of the celebration.

BIRTHDAYS

- LYLE AND THE BIRTHDAY PARTY, by Ira Waber (Houghton Mifflin). The famous character is green with envy in this tale.

- ALICE AND THE BIRTHDAY GIANT, written by John F. Green and illustrated by Maryann Kovalski (Scholastic). Be careful what you wish for.

- THE CASE OF THE MISSING BIRTHDAY PARTY, written by Joanne Rocklin and illustrated by John Speirs (Scholastic Hello Math Reader Level 4); digits and place value.

LYLE AND THE BIRTHDAY PARTY. Reprinted by permission of Houghton Mifflin.

FAMILY

- NANA UPSTAIRS & NANA DOWNSTAIRS, by Tomie dePaola (Putnam); the love between the young and the old, and accepting death.

- WALKING WITH MAGA, written by Maureen Boyd Biro and illustrated by Joyce Wheeler (All About Kids). A child walks with her grandmother through the seasons.

- MY GREAT-AUNT ARIZONA, written by Gloria Houston and illustrated by Susan Condie Lamb (HarperCollins); a great-aunt who was also a great teacher.

- SONG AND DANCE MAN, written by Karen Ackerman and illustrated by Stephen Gammell (Knopf); Caldecott Medal. Grandpa relives the good old days of vaudeville with his grandchildren in the attic during the hour before supper.

- WHISTLING, written by Elizabeth Partridge and illustrated by Anna Grossnickle Hines (Greenwillow); see the read-aloud plan.

- DAWN, by Uri Shulevitz (Farrar, Straus & Giroux). A boy and his grandfather camp and rise at dawn.

- CHERRIES AND CHERRY PITS, by Vera B. Williams (Greenwillow). The families in this young artist's mind eat cherries and spit out the pits.

- A CHAIR FOR MY MOTHER, by Vera B. Williams (Greenwillow). A girl and her mother buy a new chair from her mom's waitressing tips after a fire destroys their home.

- NOW ONE FOOT, NOW THE OTHER, by Tomie dePaola (Putnam); a tender story about the bond between a boy and his grandfather, who teach each other to walk.

- THROUGH GRANDPA'S EYES, written by Patricia MacLachlan and illustrated by Deborah Kogan Ray (HarperCollins); a touching story about a special relationship between a grandchild and Grandpa, who is blind.

- A BEAUTIFUL PEARL, written by Nancy Whitelaw and illustrated by Judith Friedman (Whitman). A grandmother with Alzheimer's remembers her granddaughter's birthday.

- THE MOTHER'S DAY MICE, written by Eve Bunting and illustrated by Jan Brett (Clarion); see the read-aloud plan.

- THE COFFEE CAN KID, written by Jan M. Czech and illustrated by Maurie J. Manning (Child and Family Press); foreign adoption; the see read-aloud plan.

- THE WHITE SWAN EXPRESS: A STORY ABOUT ADOPTION, written by Jean Davies Okimoto and Elaine M. Aoki, illustrated by Meilo So (Clarion).

- HAPPY ADOPTION DAY!, lyrics by John McCutcheon, illustrated by Julie Paschkis (Little, Brown).

- TELL ME AGAIN ABOUT THE NIGHT I WAS BORN, written by Jamie Lee Curtis and illustrated by Laura Cornell (HarperCollins); an adoption story.

- OVER THE MOON: AN ADOPTION TALE, by Karen Katz (Holt).

- THANKSGIVING AT THE TAPPLETONS', written by Eileen Spinelli and illustrated by Maryann Cocca-Leffler (Addison-Wesley; HarperCollins); see the read-aloud plan.

- THE MEMORY CUPBOARD: A THANKSGIVING STORY, written by Charlotte Herman and illustrated by Ben F. Stahl (Whitman). Katie learns that it is people, not things, that make memories.

- THE BORROWED HANUKKAH LATKES, written by Linda Glaser and illustrated by Nancy Cote (Whitman); see the read-aloud plan.

- INSIDE-OUT GRANDMA A HANUKKAH STORY, by Joan Rothenberg (Hyperion); a delightful cumulative story; includes a recipe for latkes.

- AMAZING GRACE, written by Mary Hoffman and illustrated by Caroline Binch (Dial); see the read-aloud plan.

- SPINKY SULKS, by William Steig (Farrar, Straus & Giroux). He sulks and he sulks and he sulks, and then when he wants to make up, Spinky devises a plan; wry humor in words and pictures.

- SYLVESTER AND THE MAGIC PEBBLE, by William Steig (Aladdin); Caldecott Medal; selected as one of the 100 Best Books of the Century by the National Education Association; the story of a reunited family and their undying love for one another.

- HOME AT LAST, written by Susan Middleton Elya and illustrated by Felipe Davalos (Lee & Low); see the read-aloud plan.

- UNCLE MAGIC, written by Patricia Lee Gauch and illustrated by Deborah Kogan Ray (Holiday House); about an uncle and magic and the power of opening your heart and believing.

- WHEN LIGHTNING COMES IN A JAR, by Patricia Polacco (Philomel). You're invited to a Polacco-style family reunion, filled with traditions, memories, and something new.

- ZARA'S HATS, by Paul Meisel (Dutton). Zara saves the day when her father, the hatmaker, runs out of feathers.

- ZELDA AND IVY: THREE STORIES ABOUT THE FABULOUS FOX SISTERS, by Laura McGee Kvasnosky (Candlewick); see the read-aloud plan.

- ZELDA AND IVY AND THE BOY NEXT DOOR and ZELDA AND IVY ONE CHRISTMAS, by Laura McGee Kvasnosky (Candlewick); more sisterly adventures.

- DABBLE DUCK, written by Anne Leo Ellis and illustrated by Sue Truesdell (HarperCollins); see the read-aloud plan.

- THE ONE IN THE MIDDLE IS THE GREEN KANGAROO, written by Judy Blume and illustrated by Amy Aitken (Bradbury); see the read-aloud plan.

- THE PAIN AND THE GREAT ONE, written by Judy Blume and illustrated by Irene Trivas (Bradbury); sibling rivalry in a story told from the points of view of both the older sister and the younger brother.

- UNCLE ANDY'S, by James Warhola (Putnam); see the read-aloud plan.

- KNOTS ON A COUNTING ROPE, written by Bill Martin Jr. and John Archambault and illustrated by Ted Rand (Holt); see the read-aloud plan.

- ORANGES ON GOLD MOUNTAIN, written by Elizabeth Partridge and illustrated by Aki Sogabe (Penguin). A Chinese boy makes his home on the California coast in the 1850s.

- ALL THE PLACES TO LOVE, written by Patricia MacLachlan and illustrated by Mike Wimmer (HarperCollins); lush illustrations. All the places that touch one's heart make us who we are and connect us to those who are special to us.

- THE SEA CHEST, written by Toni Buzzeo and illustrated by Mary GrandPre (Dial); lush oil paintings by the illustrator of the Harry Potter books accompany a lyrical legend of coastal Maine.

- CHICKEN SUNDAY, by Patricia Polacco (Philomel); Children's Choice and ALA Notable Book about differences, friendship, and character.

- THE TICKY-TACKY DOLL, written by Cynthia Rylant and illustrated by Harvey Stevenson (Harcourt). A reluctant child's grandmother helps ease the transition to school.

- OWL MOON, written by Jane Yolen and illustrated by John Schoenherr (Philomel); see the read-aloud plan in *Children's Book Corner, Pre-K–K*.

PETS

- DABBLE DUCK, written by Anne Leo Ellis and illustrated by Sue Truesdell (HarperCollins); see the read-aloud plan.

- PET OF A PET, by Marsha Hayles, illustrated by Scott Nash (Dial); delightful circular tale (no pun intended!)

- MADLENKA'S DOG, by Peter Sis (Farrar Straus & Giroux); an outstanding lift-the-flap book celebrating imagination.

- MY DOG IS LOST!, by Ezra Jack Keats and Pat Cherr (Puffin Books); classic Keats.

- MARTHA CALLING; MARTHA BLAH BLAH; MARTHA WALKS THE DOG; MARTHA SPEAKS, by Susan Meddaugh (Houghton Mifflin). This pup eats alphabet soup and the fun begins!

- HARRY'S DOG, written by Barbara Ann Porte and illustrated by Yossi Abolafia (Greenwillow); a beginning reader about a dog who makes Dad sneeze and the boy who comes up with a plan to keep Dad, his pup, and himself happy.

- DOG EARED, by Amanda Harvey (Doubleday). This book stars sweet, adorable, big-eared Otis, who is taunted by a bully twice. The first time is much worse than the second.

- PINKERTON, BEHAVE!, by Steven Kellogg (Dial). This Great Dane isn't so great at learning commands, much to the delight of readers, who will want to linger over these comical illustrations.

- "LET'S GET A PUP!" SAID KATE, by Bob Graham (Candlewick); delightful award winner.

- GO HOME! THE TRUE STORY OF JAMES THE CAT, by Libby Phillips Meggs (Whitman); a gentle story based on true events about a stray cat.

- I'LL ALWAYS LOVE YOU, by Hans Wilhelm (Crown); the loss of a pet and the lessons it brings.

- THE TENTH GOOD THING ABOUT BARNEY, written by Judith Viorst and illustrated by Erik Blegvad (Atheneum); see the read-aloud plan.

- THE STRAY DOG, by Marc Simont (HarperCollins); Caldecott Honor. A dog finds his home.

- THE MYSTERIOUS TADPOLE, by Steven Kellogg (Dial); award-winning tale about Louis's birthday gift: a "tadpole" from Uncle McAllister, who lives in Scotland near Loch Ness.

- ROTTEN RALPH, written by Jack Gantos and illustrated by Nicole Rubel (Houghton Mifflin); a series of books about one irascible feline!

- MRS. PEACHTREE AND THE EIGHTH AVENUE CAT, written by Erica Silverman and illustrated by Ellen Beier (Aladdin). She won't admit it, but Mrs. Peachtree has adopted this stray.

- CHARLIE ANDERSON, written by Barbara Abercrombie and illustrated by Mark Graham (Whitman). This cat has two homes; gorgeous illustrations.

- MR. POTTER'S PET, written by Dick King-Smith and illustrated by Mark Teague (Hyperion); see the read-aloud plan.

- CATWINGS, written by Ursula K. LeGuin and illustrated by S. D. Schindler (Orchard); fantasy; see the read-aloud plan.

- FISH FOR YOU: CARING FOR YOUR FISH, written by Susan Blackaby and illustrated by Charlene DeLage (Picture Window Books); nonfiction.

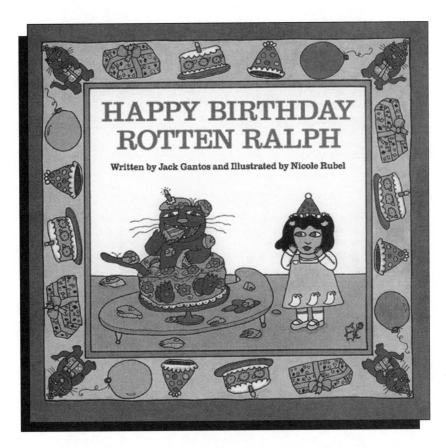

HAPPY BIRTHDAY ROTTEN RALPH. Reprinted by permission of Houghton Mifflin.

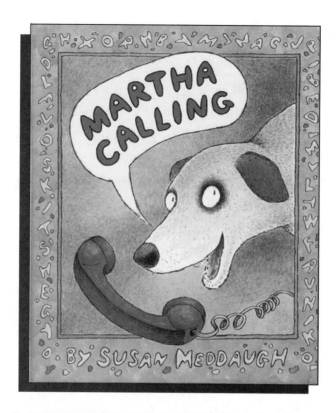

MARTHA CALLING. Reprinted by permission of Houghton Mifflin.

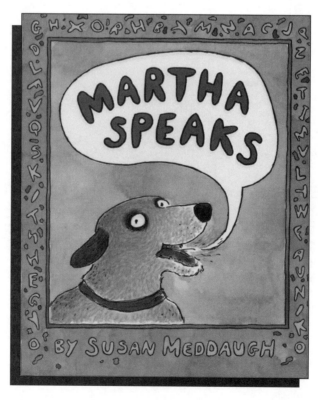

MARTHA SPEAKS. Reprinted by permission of Houghton Mifflin.

FRIENDSHIP

- THE HATING BOOK, written by Charlotte Zolotow and illustrated by Ben Shecter (HarperCollins); about misunderstandings.

- HOW TO LOSE ALL YOUR FRIENDS, by Nancy Carlson (Penguin); simple text lists six things to do, with instructions.

- SWEET BRIAR GOES TO SCHOOL, written by Karma Wilson and illustrated by LeUyen Pham (Dial). A skunk helps her classmates see beyond their noses.

- GEORGE AND MARTHA, by James Marshall (Houghton Mifflin); "five stories about two great friends" in picture book format.

- COCK-A-DOODLE DUDLEY, by Bill Peet (Houghton Mifflin); see the read-aloud plan.

- HALLO-WIENER, by Dav Pilkey (Scholastic); see the read-aloud plan.

- STELLALUNA, by Janell Cannon (Harcourt); see the read-aloud plan.

- THE OTHER SIDE, written by Jacqueline Woodson and illustrated by E. B. Lewis (Putnam); see the read-aloud plan.

- CHICKEN SUNDAY, by Patricia Polacco (Philomel); Children's Choice and ALA Notable Book about differences and friendship.

- THE DOORBELL RANG, by Pat Hutchins (Greenwillow); see the read-aloud plan.

- IRA SLEEPS OVER, by Bernard Waber (Houghton Mifflin); see the read-aloud plan.

- LOOKING OUT FOR SARAH, by Glenna Lang (Charlesbridge); the story of a guide dog, based on fact.

- I'M NOT INVITED?, by Diana Cain Bluthenthal (Atheneum); see the read-aloud plan.

- FROM ME TO YOU, written by Anthony France and illustrated by Tiphanie Beeke (Candlewick). From the bathrobe blues to a party for friends, one kind letter can make all the difference.

- FOUR VALENTINES IN A RAINSTORM, by Felicia Bond (HarperCollins); a perfect picture book.

GEORGE AND MARTHA. Reprinted by permission of Houghton Mifflin.

SCHOOL

- FIRST DAY JITTERS, written by Julie Danneberg and illustrated by Judy Love (Charlesbridge). Even the teacher has first day jitters!; clever plot.

- FIRST DAY, HOORAY!, by Nancy Poydar (Holiday House). All the players, from the bus driver to the children, get ready in their own way for the first day of school.

- THE KISSING HAND, by Audrey Penn, illustrated by Ruth E. Harper and Nancy M. Leak (Child Welfare League of America); reassurance and support from a loving mother to a reluctant child.

- THE TICKY-TACKY DOLL, written by Cynthia Rylant and illustrated by Harvey Stevenson (Harcourt). A reluctant child's grandmother helps ease the transition to school.

- SUMI'S FIRST DAY OF SCHOOL EVER, written by Soyung Pak and illustrated by Joung Un Kim (Viking); a child's first day of school in a new country.

- SCHOOL PICTURE DAY, written by Lynn Plourde and illustrated by Thor Wickstrom (Dutton); hilarious.

- TODAY WAS A TERRIBLE DAY, written by Patricia Reilly Giff and illustrated by Susanna Natti (Viking); see the read-aloud plan.

- LILLY'S PURPLE PLASTIC PURSE, by Kevin Henkes (Greenwillow); a fabulously wise teacher as seen through the eyes of the popular young diva, Lilly.

- AXLE ANNIE, written by Robin Pulver and illustrated by Tedd Arnold (Puffin); see the read-aloud plan.

- STUART GOES TO SCHOOL, written by Sara Pennypacker and illustrated by Martin Matje (Orchard); sequel to STUART'S CAPE.

- A BUS OF OUR OWN, written by Freddi Williams Evans and illustrated by Shawn Costello (Whitman); a story based on real events about an African-American community that, in the pre-civil rights era, works together to get a bus to take their children to school.

- OFFICER BUCKLE AND GLORIA, by Peggy Rathmann (Putnam); see the read-aloud plan.

- MISS SMITH'S INCREDIBLE STORYBOOK, by Michael Garland (Dutton); see the read-aloud plan.

- STAND TALL, MOLLY LOU MELON, written by Patty Lovell and illustrated by David Catrow (Putnam); see the read-aloud plan.

- THE RECESS QUEEN, written by Alexis O"Neill and illustrated by Laura Huliska-Beith (Scholastic); familiarly rotten, but reformable.

- AMAZING GRACE, written by Mary Hoffman and illustrated by Caroline Binch (Dial); see the read-aloud plan.

- RUBY THE COPYCAT, by Peggy Rathmann (Scholastic); see the read-aloud plan.

- THE HERO OF THIRD GRADE, written by Alice DeLaCroix and illustrated by Cynthia Fisher (Holiday House).

- SPIDER STORCH'S FUMBLED FIELD TRIP, written by Gina Willner-Pardo and illustrated by Nick Sharratt (Whitman); a field trip to remember; chapter book.

- DOUBLE BUBBLE TROUBLE!, written by Judy Bradbury and illustrated by Cathy Trachok (McGraw-Hill). Christopher gets in trouble for chewing gum in class and works out a way to blow his troubles away; counting by twos.

Cover of SPIDER STORCH'S FUMBLED FIELD TRIP, copyright 1998 illustrated by Nick Sharratt, used with permission of Albert Whitman and Company.

CONFLICT

- STAND TALL, MOLLY LOU MELON, written by Patty Lovell and illustrated by David Catrow (Putnam); see the read-aloud plan.

- TYRONE THE HORRIBLE, by Hans Wilhelm (Scholastic). Wilhelm's illustrations extend the story.

- TYRONE THE DOUBLE DIRTY ROTTEN CHEATER. by Hans Wilhelm (Scholastic); more antics from the irascible Tyrone.

- THE RECESS QUEEN, written by Alexis O'Neill and illustrated by Laura Huliska-Beith (Scholastic); look beyond appearances.

- LOUD-MOUTHED GEORGE AND THE SIXTH-GRADE BULLY, by Nancy Carlson (Carolrhoda); a classic.

- BULLY TROUBLE, written by Joanna Cole and illustrated by Marylin Hafner (Random House); a Step into Reading, Step 2 beginning reader.

- SWEET BRIAR GOES TO SCHOOL, written by Karma Wilson and illustrated by LeUyen Pham (Dial). Although Briar smells skunky, she wins over her classmates.

- DOG EARED, by Amanda Harvey (Doubleday); name-calling resolution at its best.

- COCK-A-DOODLE-DUDLEY, by Bill Peet (Houghton Mifflin); see the read-aloud plan.

- RUBY THE COPYCAT, by Peggy Rathmann (Scholastic); see the read-aloud plan.

FAIRY TALES, FABLES, FOLK TALES, LEGENDS, AND TALL TALES

- THE PRINCESS AND THE PEA, adapted and illustrated by Janet Stevens (Holiday House). This princess is a tigress, and the court is equally cuddly cats.

- GOLDILOCKS AND THE THREE BEARS, retold and illustrated by James Marshall (Dial); Caldecott Honor.

- HANSEL AND GRETEL, retold and illustrated by James Marshall (Dial).

- RED RIDING HOOD, retold and illustrated by James Marshall (Dial); a reassuring ending.

- LON PO PO: A RED-RIDING HOOD STORY FROM CHINA, translated and illustrated by Ed Young (Putnam); Caldecott Medal.

- MISS SMITH'S INCREDIBLE STORYBOOK, by Michael Garland (Dutton); psee the read-aloud plan.

- WHO'S AFRAID OF THE BIG BAD BOOK?, by Lauren Child (Hyperion). Herb falls asleep on his book—or rather falls into his book—and the adventure begins.

Cover of WHO'S AFRAID OF THE BIG BAD BOOK?, copyright 2002 by Lauren Child, reprinted with permission of Hyperion Books for Children.

- GOLDIE LOCKS HAS CHICKEN POX, written by Erin Dealey and illustrated by Hanako Wakiyama (Atheneum). Storybook and nursery rhyme characters visit Goldie Locks and her terrible-teaser-of-a-brother as she recuperates from chicken pox.

- STELLA LOUELLA'S RUNAWAY BOOK, by Lisa Campbell Ernst (Simon & Schuster). An array of characters who have read Louella's missing library book join in her search to recover it. Gather the clues to discover which much-loved tale the book is about.

- EACH PEACH PEAR PLUM, by Janet Ahlberg and Allan Ahlberg (Puffin); see the read-aloud plan in *Children's Book Corner Pre-K–K* .

- THE NIGHTINGALE, retold by Stephen Mitchell and illustrated by Bagram Ibatoulline (Candlewick). Breathtaking illustrations accompany the well-crafted text of this often-told Andersen tale.

- THE TALE OF THE MANDARIN DUCKS, written by Katherine Paterson and illustrated by Leo Dillon and Diane Dillon (Penguin). Kindness and love win out over troubles borne.

- THE TALKING EGGS, written by Robert D. San Souci and illustrated by Jerry Pinkney (Dial); Caldecott Honor. Adapted from a Creole folk tale, this is a blend of Cinderella and other European fairy tales in which the honest, kind sister prevails over the evil sister and mother.

- THE PAPER DRAGON, written by Marguerite W. Davol and illustrated by Robert Sabuda (Atheneum). Gatefold illustrations cut from painted tissue paper and adhered to handmade Japanese paper accompany this Chinese tale of a humble, loving scrollmaker and what he teaches a malevolent dragon; Golden Kite Award.

- THE THREE SILLIES, retold and illustrated by Kathryn Hewitt (Harcourt). Lush watercolor and gouache illustrations accompany this silly, silly, silly story.

- CLEVER BEATRICE, written by Margaret Willey and illustrated by Heather Solomon (Atheneum); see the read-aloud plan.

- CLEVER TOM AND THE LEPRECHAUN, retold and illustrated by Linda Shute (HarperCollins); lively illustrations of a spry character.

- CHICKEN LITTLE, retold and illustrated by Steven Kellogg (HarperCollins). You'll find it hard to resist reading this version in which the foxy lady sports shades and a serious set of chops, and the turkey pumps iron at Big Bozo's Barnyard Gym.

- FABLES, by Arnold Lobel (HarperCollins); Caldecott Medal.

- AESOP'S FABLES, retold and illustrated by Brad Sneed (Dial). Fifteen tales (plus a 16th one told between the covers), illustrated from an up close, in-your-face perspective, are sure to please contemporary listeners.

- THE ROUGH-FACE GIRL, written by Rafe Martin and illustrated by David Shannon (Putnam); see the read-aloud plan.

- PRINCESS FURBALL, retold by Charlotte Huck and illustrated by Anita Lobel (HarperCollins); a variant of the Cinderella story in which the princess is smart and resourceful.

- MUFARO'S BEAUTIFUL DAUGHTERS: AN AFRICAN TALE, retold and illustrated by John Steptoe (HarperCollins); Caldecott Honor; kindness triumphs.

- BIGFOOT CINDERRRRRELLA, written by Tony Johnston and illustrated by James Warhola (Putnam). Cinderella is a member of a "band of Bigfoots" and a grizzly is her "beary godfather"; grrrrrreat!

- FREDERICK, by Leo Lionni (Random House). A mouse's poetic words lighten and brighten dreary winter for his field mice friends.

- TURTLE'S RACE WITH BEAVER, told by Joseph Bruchac and James Bruchac and illustrated by Jose Aruego and Ariane Dewey (Dial); a tortoise and the hare tale adapted from Seneca oral tradition.

- RAVEN: A TRICKSTER TALE FROM THE PACIFIC NORTHWEST, told and illustrated by Gerald McDermott (Harcourt); Caldecott Honor; tale of a figure that is central to tribal arts of the Pacific Northwest.

- THE STORY OF FROG BELLY RAT BONE, by Timothy Basil Ering (Candlewick); see the read-aloud plan.

- MY LUCKY DAY, by Keiko Kasza (Putnam); see the read-aloud plan.

- STONE SOUP, written by Ann McGovern and illustrated by Winslow Pinney Pels (Scholastic). Engaging illustrations accompany this tale retold for beginning readers.

- JOHNNY APPLESEED, retold and illustrated by Steven Kellogg (HarperCollins); delightful, action-packed spreads.

- PECOS BILL, retold and illustrated by Steven Kellogg (HarperCollins). This story of a Texan hero is appealing in every way.

- MIKE FINK, retold and illustrated by Steven Kellogg (HarperCollins); a tall tale about "the most famous of the ring-tailed roarers and river wrestlers" in America's frontier history.

- PAUL BUNYAN, retold and illustrated by Steven Kellogg (HarperCollins); spunky illustrations of one of the most beloved of tall-tale heroes.

- THE LEGEND OF BLUEBONNET, retold and illustrated by Tomie dePaola (Putnam); a tale of the flower of Texas.

- ORANGES ON GOLD MOUNTAIN, written by Elizabeth Partridge and illustrated by Aki Sogabe (Penguin). A Chinese boy makes his home on the California coast in the 1850s.

- THE SEA CHEST, written by Toni Buzzeo and illustrated by Mary GrandPre (Dial). Lush oil paintings accompany a lyrical legend of coastal Maine.

Fractured Fairy Tales

- THE THREE LITTLE WOLVES AND THE BIG BAD PIG, written by Eugene Trivizas and illustrated by Helen Oxenbury (Macmillan). The pig's the bad guy here.

- RUMPELSTILTSKIN'S DAUGHTER, written and illustrated by Diane Stanley (Morrow). Her name is Hope, and she's strong and smart.

- JIM AND THE BEANSTALK, by Raymond Briggs (Putnam). Jim earns gold coins by helping the old giant feel young again.

- THE TRUE STORY OF THE 3 LITTLE PIGS!, by Jon Scieszka, illustrated by Lane Smith (Viking); hilarious; popular title in this subgenre.

- THE THREE PIGS, by David Wiesner (Clarion). This creatively illustrated retelling won the Caldecott Award.

- THE THREE SPINNING FAIRIES: A TALE FROM THE BROTHERS GRIMM, retold by Lisa Campbell Ernst (Dutton). Lazy, selfish Zelda cooks up a scheme and gets her just desserts.

- GOLDILOCKS RETURNS, by Lisa Campbell Ernst (Simon & Schuster). A grown-up Goldilocks, armed with a tool belt, opinions, and unlimited energy, returns to the scene of the crime to make things right.

Text and illustrations copyright © 2001 STELLA LOUELLA'S RUNAWAY BOOK written and illustrated by Lisa Campbell Ernst. Used with permission of Aladdin Paperbacks, an imprint of Simon & Schuster Children's Publishing.

THE ARTS

- HANDEL WHO KNEW WHAT HE LIKED, written by M. T. Anderson and illustrated by Kevin Hawkes (Candlewick); a Boston Globe–Horn Book Honor Award for Nonfiction.

- BEETHOVEN LIVES UPSTAIRS, written by Barbara Nichol and illustrated by Scott Cameron (Orchard); letters between Christoph and his uncle about the "madman" who moves into the upstairs office in the home that Christoph and his mother occupy.

- PIECES A YEAR IN POEMS & QUILTS, by Anna Grossnickle Hines (HarperCollins); poems illustrated with quilts; includes afterword on the story behind the quilts.

- HATTIE AND THE WILD WAVES, by Barbara Cooney (Penguin); about a girl who loves to paint; written and illustrated by the Caldecott Medal winner.

- UNCLE ANDY'S, by James Warhola (Putnam); about Andy Warhol; see the read-aloud plan.

- THE DINOSAURS OF WATERHOUSE HAWKINS, written by Barbara Kerley and illustrated by Brian Selznick (Scholastic); see the read-aloud plan.

- ACTION JACKSON, by Jan Greenberg and Sandra Jordan, illustrated by Robert Andrew Parker (Roaring Brook Press); about Jackson Pollock.

- TALKING WITH ARTISTS, compiled and edited by Pat Cummings (Bradbury); an excellent reference book for children in which children's book illustrators answer questions about where they get ideas, what their work day is like, and how they make their pictures. Artists highlighted include Chris Van Allsburg, Tom Feelings, David Wiesner, Lane Smith, Leo Dillon and Diane Dillon, and Lisa Campbell Ernst.

- MATH-TERPIECES, written by Greg Tang and illustrated by Greg Paprocki (Scholastic); see the read-aloud plan.

- THE PHILHARMONIC GETS DRESSED, written by Karla Kuskin and illustrated by Marc Simont (HarperCollins); see the read-aloud plan.

- ZIN! ZIN! ZIN! A VIOLIN, written by Lloyd Moss and illustrated by Marjorie Priceman (Aladdin). Ten pieces of the orchestra are described in rhyme and led by a fanciful conductor; a Caldecott Honor book.

JUDY MOODY GETS FAMOUS! Text © 2001 by Megan McDonald. Illustrations © 2001 by Fablevision, LLC/Peter Reynolds. Reproduced by permission of the publisher Candlewick Press, Inc., Cambridge, MA.

SONG-RELATED BOOKS

- THE ITSY BITSY SPIDER, as told and illustrated by Iza Trapani (Whispering Coyote Press).

- THERE WAS AN OLD LADY WHO SWALLOWED A FLY, by Simms Taback (Viking); Caldecott Honor Award.

- GETTING TO KNOW YOU!, Rogers and Hammerstein Favorites illustrated by Rosemary Wells (HarperCollins); seventeen songs, signature illustrations; includes songbook.

- HAPPY ADOPTION DAY!, lyrics by John McCutcheon, illustrated by Julie Paschkis (Little, Brown).

- HOW MUCH IS THAT DOGGIE IN THE WINDOW?, words and music by Bob Merrill; retold and illustrated by Iza Trapani (Whispering Coyote).

- THE FARMER IN THE DELL, edited by Ann Owen and illustrated by Sandra D'Antonio (Picture Window Books).

- THE STORY OF THE STAR-SPANGLED BANNER, written by Steven Kroll and illustrated by Dan Andreasen (Scholastic).

- YANKEE DOODLE: A SONG FROM THE AMERICAN REVOLUTION, illustrated by Todd Ouren (Picture Window Books).

- THE FRIENDLY BEASTS, illustrated by Tomie dePaola (Putnam); old English Christmas carol.

- WE WISH YOU A MERRY CHRISTMAS, illustrated by Tracey Campbell Pearson (Dial).

- THE LITTLE DRUMMER BOY, words and music by Katherine Davis, Henry Onorati, and Harry Simeone; illustrated by Ezra Jack Keats (Macmillan).

- HANUKKAH LIGHTS, HANUKKAH NIGHTS, written by Leslie Kimmelman and illustrated by John Himmelman (HarperCollins); interactive press-the-button book includes "My Little Dreidel."

WRITING

- CLICK, CLACK, MOO: COWS THAT TYPE, written by Doreen Cronin and illustrated by Betsy Lewin (Simon & Schuster); see the read-aloud plan.

- DEAR MRS. LARUE: LETTERS FROM OBEDIENCE SCHOOL, by Mark Teague (Scholastic); see the read-aloud plan.

- PUNCTUATION TAKES A VACATION, written by Robin Pulver and illustrated by Lynn Rowe Reed (Holiday House); see the read-aloud plan.

- THE JOLLY POSTMAN OR OTHER PEOPLE'S LETTERS, by Janet Ahlberg and Allan Ahlberg (Little, Brown). Well-known fairy tale characters get mail.

- THE JOLLY POCKET POSTMAN, by Janet Ahlberg and Allan Ahlberg (Little, Brown).

- THE JOLLY CHRISTMAS POSTMAN, by Janet Ahlberg and Allan Ahlberg (Little, Brown).

- ANGELINA BALLERINA'S INVITATION TO THE BALLET, written by Katharine Holabird and illustrated by Helen Craig (Pleasant Company); includes pull-out letters and a poster.

- DEAR ANNIE, by Judith Caseley (Greenwillow). Letters between a girl and her grandpa chronicle events in her childhood.

- BEETHOVEN LIVES UPSTAIRS, written by Barbara Nichol and illustrated by Scott Cameron (Orchard Books); correspondence between a boy and his uncle about the "madman" who lives upstairs.

- WRITE UP A STORM WITH THE POLK STREET SCHOOL, written by Patricia Reilly Giff and illustrated by Blanche Sims (Dell); an outstanding how-to, using examples from the popular Kids of the Polk Street School series to illustrate writing concepts and techniques; appropriate for second grade and beyond.

- FREDERICK, by Leo Lionni (Random House). A mouse's poetic words lighten and brighten dreary winter for his field mice friends.

- THE AMAZING POP-UP GRAMMAR BOOK, by Jennie Maizels and Kate Petty (Dutton); a book that lives up to its name.

- ROSES ARE PINK, YOUR FEET REALLY STINK, by Diane de Groat (HarperCollins). Gilbert writes naughty and nice poems on his Valentine's Day cards.

- THANK YOU, SANTA, written by Margaret Wild and illustrated by Kerry Argent (Omnibus Books); letters throughout the year between a girl and Santa.

- FROM ME TO YOU, written by Anthony France and illustrated by Tiphanie Beeke (Candlewick). From the bathrobe blues to a party for friends, one kind letter can make all the difference.

• THE GARDENER, written by Sarah Stewart and illustrated by David Small (Farrar, Straus & Giroux); Caldecott Honor; letters between a girl and her folks during the Depression.

THE JUDY MOODY MOOD JOURNAL. Text Copyright © 2003 by Megan McDonald. Illustrations Copyright © 2003 by Peter H. Reynolds. Judy Moody font Copyright © 2003 by Peter H. Reynolds. Reproduced by permission of the publisher Candlewick Press, Inc., Cambridge, MA.

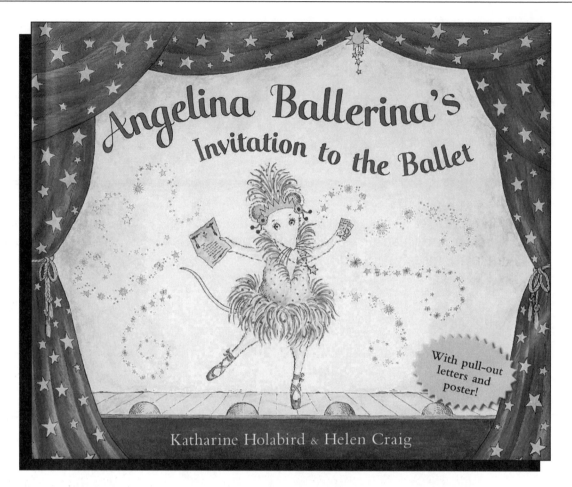

MATH

- MATH-TERPIECES, written by Greg Tang and illustrated by Greg Paprocki (Scholastic); see the read-aloud plan.

- MATH FOR ALL SEASONS, written by Greg Tang and illustrated by Harry Briggs (Scholastic); math riddle poems involving addition, subtracting to add, and patterns.

- THE DOORBELL RANG, by Pat Hutchins (Greenwillow); see the read-aloud plan.

- ONE CARTON OF OOPS!, written by Judy Bradbury and illustrated by Cathy Trachok (McGraw-Hill). Christopher is sent to the store for a carton of eggs and his troubles begin; concept of a dozen; subtraction.

- DOUBLE BUBBLE TROUBLE!, written by Judy Bradbury and illustrated by Cathy Trachok (McGraw-Hill). Christopher gets in trouble for chewing gum in class and works out a way to blow his troubles away; counting by twos.

- THE FLY ON THE CEILING: A MATH MYTH, written by Dr. Julie Glass and illustrated by Richard Walz (Random House); Scholastic Step into Reading and Math Step 3; graphing and coordinates.

- THE CASE OF THE MISSING BIRTHDAY PARTY, written by Joanne Rocklin and illustrated by John Speirs (Scholastic Hello Math Reader Level 4); digits and place value.

- HOW MUCH IS THAT GUINEA PIG IN THE WINDOW?, written by Joanne Rocklin and illustrated by Meredith Johnson (Scholastic Hello Math Reader Level 4); money, addition, multiplication, calculation.

- A HIGH-FIVING GIFT FOR MOM!, written by Judy Bradbury and illustrated by Cathy Trachok (McGraw-Hill). Christopher and his brothers go to a teachers' craft fair to buy a gift for Mother's Day.

- HOW MUCH IS A MILLION?, written by David M. Schwartz and illustrated by Steven Kellogg (HarperCollins); counting, comparing, quantifying to explain the enormity of a million, a billion, and a trillion.

- EATING FRACTIONS, by Bruce McMillan (Scholastic). A meal is shared by two kids and a dog to introduce the concept of fractions; with photographs.

- DOGGONE LEMONADE STAND!, written by Judy Bradbury and illustrated by Cathy Trachok (McGraw-Hill). Christopher sets up a lemonade stand on the hottest day of the year; simple fractions.

- THE PHILHARMONIC GETS DRESSED, written by Karla Kuskin and illustrated by Marc Simont (HarperCollins); see the read-aloud plan.

- MATH CURSE, written by Jon Scieszka and illustrated by Lane Smith (Viking); zany, zesty, zippy fun, fun, fun, by the masterful duo.

- ALEXANDER, WHO USED TO BE RICH LAST SUNDAY, written by Judith Viorst and illustrated by Ray Cruz (Aladdin). There's so much you could do with a dollar!

A SENSE OF PLACE; HISTORY

• WHEN I WAS YOUNG IN THE MOUNTAINS, written by Cynthia Rylant and illustrated by Diane Goode (Dutton); a memoir of growing up in Appalachia; Caldecott Honor and Reading Rainbow Book selection.

• OX-CART MAN, written by Donald Hall and illustrated by Barbara Cooney (Viking); the life in seasons of a pioneer farmer and his family; Caldecott Medal.

• THE GARDENER, written by Sarah Stewart and illustrated by David Small (Farrar, Straus & Giroux); Caldecott Honor; letters between a girl and her folks during the Depression.

• ALL THE PLACES TO LOVE, written by Patricia MacLachlan and illustrated by Mike Wimmer (HarperCollins); lush illustrations. The places that touch our hearts make us who we are and connect us to those we love.

• A MOON IN MY TEACUP, by Anita Riggio (Boyds Mills Press); nostalgic oil paintings. The manger scene stirs special feelings on a visit to Grandma and Grandpa's house.

• MISS RUMPHIUS, by Barbara Cooney (Viking); an aunt who travels the world and leaves something behind.

• MY GREAT-AUNT ARIZONA, written by Gloria Houston and illustrated by Susan Condie Lamb (HarperCollins). A great-aunt who was also a great teacher introduces her students to the world.

• JAPAN ABCs: A BOOK ABOUT THE PEOPLE AND PLACES OF JAPAN, written by Sarah Heiman and illustrated by Todd Ouren (Picture Window Books).

• ME ON THE MAP, written by Joan Sweeney and illustrated by Annette Cable (Crown); see the read-aloud plan.

• SARAH MORTON'S DAY: A DAY IN THE LIFE OF A PILGRIM GIRL, written by Kate Winters, with photographs by Russ Kendall (Scholastic); The story takes place in 1627. Photographed at Plimoth Plantation on Cape Cod, see the read-aloud plan.

• SAMUEL EATON'S DAY: A DAY IN THE LIFE OF A PILGRIM BOY, written by Kate Winters, with photographs by Russ Kendall (Scholastic); companion to the previous book.

• ON THE MAYFLOWER: VOYAGE OF THE SHIP'S APPRENTICE & A PASSENGER GIRL, written by Kate Winters, with photographs by Russ Kendall (Scholastic); companion to the two previous books.

• BY THE DAWN'S EARLY LIGHT: THE STORY OF THE STAR-SPANGLED BANNER, written by Steven Kroll and illustrated by Dan Andreasen (Scholastic).

See also listings in Biography.

HENRY HIKES TO FITCHBURG. Reprinted by permission of Houghton Mifflin.

HANDICAPS

- A SHOW OF HANDS: SAY IT IN SIGN LANGUAGE, written by Mary Beth Sullivan and Linda Bourke with Susan Regan and illustrated by Linda Bourke (Lippincott; Scholastic); a Reading Rainbow Book.

- HANDSIGNS: A SIGN LANGUAGE ALPHABET, by Kathleen Fain (Chronicle). Beautiful illustrations clearly depict hand signs.

- WORDS IN OUR HANDS, written by Ada B. Litchfield and illustrated by Helen Cogancherry (Whitman); a story about a family with deaf parents.

- LOOKING OUT FOR SARAH, by Glenna Lang (Charlesbridge); the story of a guide dog, based on fact.

- KNOTS ON A COUNTING ROPE, written by Bill Martin Jr. and John Archambault and illustrated by Ted Rand (Holt); see the read-aloud plan.

- THROUGH GRANDPA'S EYES, written by Patricia MacLachlan and illustrated by Deborah Kogan Ray (HarperCollins); touching story about a special relationship between a grandchild and Grandpa, who is blind.

- NAOMI KNOWS IT'S SPRINGTIME, written by Virginia L. Kroll and illustrated by Jill Kastner (Boyds Mills Press). Although she is blind, Naomi knows spring has arrived.

- JEREMY'S DREIDEL, written by Ellie Gellman and illustrated by Judith Friedman (Kar-Ben Copies). Jeremy makes a Braille dreidel for his father, who is blind.

DEATH

- NANA UPSTAIRS & NANA DOWNSTAIRS, by Tomie dePaola (Putnam); the love between the young and the old; and learning about and accepting death.

- THE TENTH GOOD THING ABOUT BARNEY, written by Judith Viorst and illustrated by Erik Blegvad (Atheneum); see the read-aloud plan.

- I'LL ALWAYS LOVE YOU, by Hans Wilhelm (Crown); the loss of a pet and the lessons it brings.

- GARDEN ANGEL, written by Jan M. Czech and illustrated by Susan Aitken (Centering Corporation). A child plants a garden as she used to with her grandfather.

- MY GRANDSON LEW, written by Charlotte Zolotow and illustrated by William Pene du Bois (HarperCollins). Lewis and his mother remember together a man they both miss.

MANNERS

- I DID IT, I'M SORRY, written by Caralyn Buehner and illustrated by Mark Buehner (Dial). Multiple-choice questions follow anecdotes meant to quiz kids on manners. Correct answers are found on the last page. Animals are concealed in the illustrations done in oil paints over acrylics.

- IT'S A SPOON, NOT A SHOVEL, written by Caralyn Buehner and illustrated by Mark Buehner (Puffin); great title, super illustrations of situations that may be silly but get the message across nevertheless; format for this book is the same as the previous one.

- EXCUSE ME!, by Lisa Kopelke (Simon & Schuster). A burping frog's problem gets bigger and badder until he remembers his manners.

- MANNERS, by Aliki (HarperCollins). Sweet illustrations accompany simple rules of etiquette.

- PERFECT PIGS, written by Marc Brown and illustrated by Stephen Krensky (Little, Brown). The title says it all.

- THE ANT AND THE ELEPHANT, by Bill Peet (Houghton Mifflin). Learn about gratitude in this story about an elephant who helps a number of ungrateful slugs out of a jam, and whose good deeds are repaid by the least likely recipient of his good deeds; see the read-aloud plan.

- MY DOG NEVER SAYS PLEASE, written by Suzanne Williams and illustrated by Tedd Arnold (Penguin). Manners are such a bother. Wouldn't it be easier to be a dog?

- COMMUNICATION, by Aliki (HarperCollins); all about talking and listening, told simply.

- WE LIVE HERE TOO! KIDS TALK ABOUT GOOD CITIZENSHIP, written by Nancy Loewen and illustrated by Omarr Wesley (Picture Window Books); inviting, humorous advice column format; discusses acting responsibly, using real-life experiences; one in a series.

- CHICKEN SUNDAY, by Patricia Polacco (Philomel); Children's Choice and ALA Notable Book about differences, friendship, and character.

DINOSAURS (FICTION AND NONFICTION)

- THE DINOSAURS OF WATERHOUSE HAWKINS, written by Barbara Kerley and illustrated by Brian Selznick (Scholastic); see the read-aloud plan.

- MY VISIT TO THE DINOSAURS, by Aliki (HarperCollins); a Let's-Read-and-Find-Out Science Book.

- DINOSAUR BOB AND HIS ADVENTURES WITH THE FAMILY LAZARDO, by William Joyce (HarperCollins); fanciful tale of Bob, the dinosaur, who comes home from a safari to live with the Lazardos in Pimlico Hills; enchanting art.

- DINOSAUR DAY; DINOSAUR GARDEN; and other titles by Liza Donnelly (Scholastic). Simple, humorous stories teach facts about these prehistoric animals.

- GIANT DINOSAURS, written by Erna Rowe and illustrated by Merle Smith (Scholastic); comparisons of dinosaurs with well-known things such as cars, houses, and living rooms.

- DINOSAURS BIG AND SMALL, written by Kathleen Weidner Zoehfeld and illustrated by Lucia Washburn (HarperCollins); a Let's-Read-and-Find-Out Science Book by the author of a number of books about dinosaurs.

- PATRICK'S DINOSAURS, written by Carol Carrick and illustrated by Donald Carrick (Houghton Mifflin). Fact and imagination blend in a story about Patrick and his big brother, Hank, who is positive there are no more dinosaurs . . .

- TIME FLIES, by Eric Rohmann (Crown); wordless wonder; Caldecott Honor.

- JACOB TWO-TWO AND THE DINOSAUR, written by Mordecai Richler and illustrated by Norman Eyolfson (Knopf). Eight year-old Jacob's in charge with the help of his friendly diplodocus, Dippy; chapter book; sequel to JACOB TWO-TWO MEETS THE HOODED FANG.

- LONG-NECK: THE ADVENTURE OF APATOSAURUS, written by Michael Dahl and illustrated by Jeff Yesh (Picture Window Books); the life cycle of this dinosaur; clear illustrations and interesting back material.

- TYRANNOSAURUS WAS A BEAST, written by Jack Prelutsky and illustrated by Arnold Lobel (Greenwillow); relates facts about the favorites in light verse.

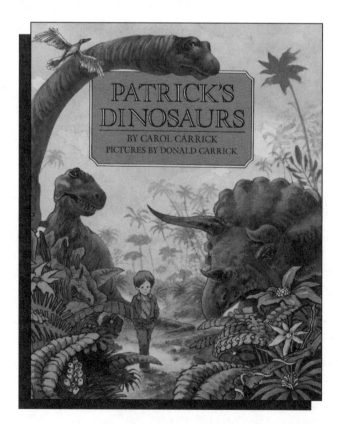

PATRICK'S DINOSAURS. Reprinted by permission of Houghton Mifflin.

ANIMALS (NONFICTION)

- ANIMALS BORN ALIVE AND WELL, by Ruth Heller (Grosset & Dunlap); see the read-aloud plan.

- CHICKENS AREN'T THE ONLY ONES, by Ruth Heller (Grosset & Dunlap); in the style of the previous book.

- WHO GROWS UP ON THE FARM? A BOOK ABOUT FARM ANIMALS AND THEIR OFFSPRING, written by Theresa Longenecker and illustrated by Melissa Carpenter (Picture Window Books); simple and straightforward with inviting art; ample back material.

- GOING ON A WHALE WATCH, by Bruce McMillan (Scholastic); simple text with drawings and photographs.

- IF YOU WERE BORN A KITTEN, written by Marion Dane Bauer and illustrated by JoEllen McAllister Stammen (Simon & Schuster). Twelve kinds of baby animals with their parents are wonderfully illustrated, the final one being the human baby.

- ONE LITTLE KITTEN, by Tana Hoban (HarperCollins); simple text with photographs.

- WOLF WATCH, written by Kay Winters and illustrated by Laura Regan (Simon & Schuster). Wolf pups are born, nurtured, and protected.

- SPINNING SPIDERS, written by Melvin Berger and illustrated by S. D. Schindler (HarperCollins); a Let's-Read-and-Find-Out Science Stage 2 title.

- DOLPHIN TALK: WHISTLES, CLICKS, AND CLAPPING JAWS, written by Wendy Pfeffer and illustrated by Helen K. Davie (HarperCollins); a Let's-Read-and-Find-Out Science Stage 2 title.

- TALE OF A TADPOLE, written by Barbara Ann Porte and illustrated by Annie Cannon (Orchard); facts within a story.

- STELLALUNA, by Janell Cannon (Harcourt); bat facts within a fictional story; see the read-aloud plan.

- BUGS FOR LUNCH, written by Margery Facklam and illustrated by Sylvia Long (Charlesbridge); simple rhyme accompanied by illustrations done in pen and ink and watercolors; teaches about creatures that munch bugs for lunch.

- LOCUST POCUS! A BOOK TO BUG YOU, written by Douglas Kaine McKelvey and illustrated by Richard Egielski (Philomel); poems not for the squeamish.

- FISH FOR YOU: CARING FOR YOUR FISH, written by Susan Blackaby and illustrated by Charlene DeLage (Picture Window Books); the care of pet fish.

- GO HOME! THE TRUE STORY OF JAMES THE CAT, by Libby Phillips Meggs (Whitman); a gentle story based on true events about a stray cat.

See also Dinosaurs listed above.

Cover of GO HOME! THE TRUE STORY OF JAMES THE CAT, copyright 2000 illustrated by Libby Phillips Meggs, used with permission of Albert Whitman and Company.

BIOGRAPHY

- HANDEL WHO KNEW WHAT HE LIKED, written by M. T. Anderson and illustrated by Kevin Hawkes (Candlewick); a Boston Globe–Horn Book Honor Award for Nonfiction.

- UNCLE ANDY'S, by James Warhola (Putnam); about Andy Warhol; see the read-aloud plan.

- THE DINOSAURS OF WATERHOUSE HAWKINS, written by Barbara Kerley and illustrated by Brian Selznick (Scholastic); dinosaur sculptor and artist; see the read-aloud plan.

- ACTION JACKSON, by Jan Greenberg and Sandra Jordan, illustrated by Robert Andrew Parker (Roaring Brook Press); about Jackson Pollock.

- TALKING WITH ARTISTS, compiled and edited by Pat Cummings (Bradbury); an excellent reference book for children. Children's book illustrators answer questions about where they get ideas, what their work day is like, and how they make their pictures. Artists highlighted include Chris Van Allsburg, Tom Feelings, David Wiesner, Lane Smith, Leo Dillon and Diane Dillon, and Lisa Campbell Ernst.

- GETTING TO KNOW YOU!, Rogers and Hammerstein favorites illustrated by Rosemary Wells (HarperCollins); seventeen songs, signature illustrations; includes songbook.

- SO YOU WANT TO BE PRESIDENT?, written by Judith St. George and illustrated by David Small (Philomel); short, humorous anecdotes about U.S. presidents; winner of the Caldecott Medal.

- SO YOU WANT TO BE AN INVENTOR?, written by Judith St. George and illustrated by David Small (Philomel); in the style of the previous book.

- THE POT THAT JUAN BUILT, written by Nancy Andrews-Goebel and illustrated by David Diaz (Lee & Low); about Juan Quezada, "premier potter in Mexico."

- HENRY HIKES TO FITCHBURG and HENRY BUILDS A CABIN, by D. B. Johnson (Houghton Mifflin); intriguing facets of Henry David Thoreau's life.

- TO FLY: THE STORY OF THE WRIGHT BROTHERS, written by Wendie C. Old and illustrated by Robert Andrew Parker (Clarion).

- MARY SMITH, by A. U'Ren (Farrar, Straus & Giroux); the story of knocker-up Mary Smith, who in the 1920s before alarm clocks were widely used, shot dried peas from a rubber tube at the windows of her clients in London to wake them for work.

- PLAYERS IN PIGTAILS, written by Shana Corey and illustrated by Rebecca Gibbon (Scholastic); fictional tale based on fact, about a young woman who played in the All-American Girls Professional Baseball League during World War II.

- ABRAHAM LINCOLN, written by Amy L. Cohn and Suzy Schmidt and illustrated by David A. Johnson (Scholastic); see the read-aloud plan.

- MARTIN'S BIG WORDS: THE LIFE OF MARTIN LUTHER KING, JR., written by Doreen Rappaport and illustrated by Bryan Collier (Hyperion); see the read-aloud plan.

- A PICTURE BOOK OF MARTIN LUTHER KING, JR., written by David Adler and illustrated by Robert Casilla (Holiday House).

- FLY HIGH! THE STORY OF BESSIE COLEMAN, written by Louise Borden and Mary Kay Kroeger and illustrated by Teresa Flavin (McElderry Books).

- WHEN MARIAN SANG, written by Pam Munoz Ryan and illustrated by Brian Selznick (Scholastic); a Robert F. Sibert Honor Book; about Marian Anderson's rise to fame in the 1930s.

- GOIN' SOMEPLACE SPECIAL, written by Patricia C. McKissack and illustrated by Jerry Pinkney (Atheneum); finding acceptance at the public library in the pre-civil rights era.

GENERAL NONFICTION

- THE REASON FOR A FLOWER, by Ruth Heller (Grosset & Dunlap); bright and colorful illustrations accompany rhyming, factual text.

- PLANTS THAT NEVER EVER BLOOM, by Ruth Heller (Putnam); in style of previous book.

- THE POPCORN BOOK, by Tomie dePaola (Holiday House); facts and recipes.

- THE CLOUD BOOK, by Tomie dePaola (Holiday House); common types of clouds and what they tell us.

- ME ON THE MAP, written by Joan Sweeney and illustrated by Annette Cable (Crown); see the read-aloud plan.

- GERMS MAKE ME SICK!, written by Melvin Berger and illustrated by Marylin Hafner (HarperCollins); a classic among the Let's-Read-and-Find-Out Science titles.

- SARAH MORTON'S DAY: A DAY IN THE LIFE OF A PILGRIM GIRL, written by Kate Winters, with photographs by Russ Kendall (Scholastic).The story takes place in 1627. Photographed at Plimoth Plantation, Cape Cod; see the read-aloud plan.

- SAMUEL EATON'S DAY: A DAY IN THE LIFE OF A PILGRIM BOY, written by Kate Winters, with photographs by Russ Kendall (Scholastic); companion to the previous book.

- ON THE MAYFLOWER: VOYAGE OF THE SHIP'S APPRENTICE & A PASSENGER GIRL, written by Kate Winters, with photographs by Russ Kendall (Scholastic); companion to the two previous books.

- BY THE DAWN'S EARLY LIGHT: THE STORY OF THE STAR-SPANGLED BANNER, written by Steven Kroll and illustrated by Dan Andreasen (Scholastic).

- A SHOW OF HANDS: SAY IT IN SIGN LANGUAGE, by Mary Beth Sullivan and Linda Bourke with Susan Regan and illustrated by Linda Bourke (Lippincott; Scholastic); a Reading Rainbow Book.

- HANDSIGNS: A SIGN LANGUAGE ALPHABET, by Kathleen Fain (Chronicle). Beautiful illustrations clearly depict hand signs.

- WORDS IN OUR HANDS, written by Ada B. Litchfield and illustrated by Helen Cogancherry (Whitman); about a family with deaf parents.

- LOOKING OUT FOR SARAH, by Glenna Lang (Charlesbridge). The story of a guide dog, based on fact.

- WRITE UP A STORM WITH THE POLK STREET SCHOOL, written by Patricia Reilly Giff and illustrated by Blanche Sims (Dell); outstanding how-to, using examples from the popular Kids of the Polk Street School series to illustrate writing concepts and techniques; appropriate for second grade and beyond.

- MANNERS, by Aliki (HarperCollins). Sweet illustrations accompany simple rules of etiquette.

- MATH-TERPIECES, written by Greg Tang and illustrated by Greg Paprocki (Scholastic); see the read-aloud plan.

- MATH FOR ALL SEASONS, written by Greg Tang and illustrated by Harry Briggs (Scholastic); math riddle poems involving addition, subtracting to add, and patterns.

- HOW MUCH IS A MILLION?, written by David M. Schwartz and illustrated by Steven Kellogg (HarperCollins); counting, comparing, quantifying a million, a billion, and a trillion.

- EATING FRACTIONS, by Bruce McMillan (Scholastic). A meal is shared by two kids and a dog to introduce the concept of fractions; with photographs.

- MATH CURSE, written by Jon Scieszka and illustrated by Lane Smith (Viking); zany, zesty, zippy fun, fun, fun, by the masterful duo.

- ROCKS HARD, SOFT, SMOOTH, AND ROUGH, written by Natalie M. Rosinsky and illustrated by Matthew John (Picture Window Books); includes ample back material.

- THE SUN, THE WIND AND THE RAIN written by Lisa Westberg Peters and illustrated by Ted Rand; Holt; basic geology parallels a story about a day at the beach building a sandcastle.

POETRY

See listings in Tips and Techniques for Teachers and Librarians (pp. 144–47).

Glossary of Book Terms

The terms listed below are used in the read-aloud plans. They are defined here for your convenience.

book jacket Heavy paper cover on a hardcover book

copyright Legal means of protecting one's work. Unless sold, this is automatic to anything written, published or unpublished, for the author's lifetime plus 50 years; copyright information is usually found on the back of the title page. Illustrations are also copyrighted, and as with written work, may not be reproduced without the written permission of the copyright holder.

dedication Statement of to whom the author and/or illustrator dedicates the book; usually found after the title page before the body of the book

double-page spread Two facing pages that share one illustration

endpapers Papers pasted or free inside the front and back covers of book; see also **flyleaves**.

flap copy Information on the inside flap of the book jacket, usually about the story, author, and illustrator

flyleaves Free endpapers inside the front and back covers of a book

gouache painting with opaque watercolors

title page Page that lists title, author, illustrator, and publisher. Often on the back of the title page is found the **copyright** information.

Subject Index

Title Index

Boldface indicates titles for which a read-aloud is included in this volume.
Underscore indicates that the book cover is presented on that page.

Author Index

Illustrator Index

Index of Resource Books
and Authors

About the Author

JUDY BRADBURY is an author and teacher. She is the author of a children's math series called Christopher Counts! published by McGraw Hill/Learning Triangle Press. She is also a frequent workshop presenter.

Judy has over 20 years of experience teaching in the public school system as well as private tutoring. A lifelong advocate of promoting reading, Judy pioneered a NYS funded summer community reading program ad developed remedial/enrichment reading and writing programs for high school students. She maintains an active membership in organizations such as the International Reading Association. A lifelong resident of the Buffalo area, she resides in East Amherst, NY with her husband, daughter, one big dog, and two cats who came for Christmas and stayed.